Not Another Pair of Shoes

Building Your Brand's Story and Purpose

*To Electra
more purpose
more passion*

Alexander Novicov

Copyright © 2021 by Alexander Novicov

Book Cover Design by way boutique agency

All rights reserved. No part of this book may be reproduced or used in any manner without written permission of the copyright owner except for the use of quotations in a book review.

ISBNs:
Paperback: 978-1-914078-96-5
eBook: 978-1-914078-97-2

Published by PublishingPush.com

*This book is dedicated to my mum and dad.
Mum, thank you for everything you have done for me.
Dad, thank you for being you.*

Contents

Chapter 1	The True Power of Marketing	1
Chapter 2	What is a Purpose Driven Brand?	9
Chapter 3	What is Storytelling?	21
Chapter 4	Focus on the Purpose	35
Chapter 5	Why Your Brain Loves Great Stories	47
Chapter 6	Building Your Brand Story (The 5 What's Framework)	57
Chapter 7	Stop Talking About the Product	71
Chapter 8	A Slogan, or an Ethos?	91
Chapter 9	Customer Loyalty Vs Brand Loyalty	99
Chapter 10	Winning Hearts	104
Chapter 11	Telling Your Brand Story	116
Chapter 12	Wired to Belong	127
Chapter 13	Don't be Boring	138
Chapter 14	How a Story Can Increase Your Sales	147

| **Chapter 15** | Brand Stories to Inspire | 157 |
| **Chapter 16** | When Walking Away is the Best Thing You Can Do | 172 |

About the Author	179
Acknowledgments	181
Further reading	183
References	184

Chapter 1

The True Power of Marketing

Surely the best place to start writing a book is in Waterstones coffee shop on Tottenham Court Road. I like this place because it's calm. I sip an Americano, watch book lovers and tourists stroll at leisure, and am surrounded by brilliant authors from around the world. In my imaginary world I have other authors in front of me: all their books, all their work and passion are here. There is something magical about it.

So, it is here that I write a book about marketing. Yet in the summer of 2017, after being in the industry for eight years, I nearly gave up marketing.

I lost my passion for it because I didn't want to manipulate people to buy more *stuff* that they did not need. Then I had a realisation. After thinking of what I would do for couple of months, I decided I did not need to quit marketing - because marketing does not have to be about manipulating people, and selling things that people don't need. Marketing can be a very good tool to make change happen. Marketing can be a *bridge* to help people make the right decision for them. Marketing can be used to make this world a better place. So, I did not quit. I changed direction.

Sometimes in life we need to know when it is time to quit, and when we need to pause, to reflect and change direction. The mentality of always 'moving forward' is glorified, and unnecessary.

There is a problem, a massive problem in this world. The problem is what marketing can achieve. It can brainwash and manipulate people, and that's what a lot of people do. They understand the power of storytelling and use it to their benefits. In this book we will critically examine what we have been taught, and how we can create great business results using authentic stories. You might think that I will share the 'secret sauce' of success in marketing – maybe it's the TikTok platform, or the new Clubhouse app, or perhaps creating a podcast is the answer. No, these are tactics. Tactics change, but the fundamentals don't. It's not about what platforms to use, it's about the mentality. The mentality is the foundation; it is how we think about something. We can try to convince a person to eat healthy all day long but if that person is not in the right head space, we will be wasting our energy. Or as we know the saying, you can lead the horse to water but you can't make it drink it, if we force it then it might drown.

When you ask an average person about what they think marketing is, most people will answer, 'Manipulation, lying, selling'. When people think of selling, most of the time they don't see it as a good thing. They think of a sleazy sales man, which is disappointing. I think a lot of people think of marketing negatively, the way they might think of smartphones and social media – as a destructive force in our midst. But we can't agree that smartphones and technology are 'destroying' our society when a smartphone can be used to connect to our loved ones living across the Atlantic Ocean, it can be used to find love, it can be used to help us find a location we are looking for, it can be used to get an uber safely – and it can, of course, be used to connect with potential customers! There is the dark side, too, like anything in life. It can be used to waste countless hours staring at the screen watching the less edifying video content found on TikTok, Instagram, and YouTube.

Marketing can be so much more than just selling a product or a service. But knowing how to market, and use marketing to make a positive change, is both really inspiring and really hard. We have to admit that negativity gets attention, and so it becomes tempting to join the bandwagon and be negative. But it is not a path to long-term success. Marketing can be used to drive change; it can be used to make people aware of different problems and solutions that people can do.

Ten years ago, if you had a great burger and great customer service, you made it - you won the customer for life. Today, people's expectations are different. They want more than just a great burger.

Yet marketing always starts with the product – the great burger. Two days ago, I was going for a drink with a mate and I suggested we go to Beer + Burger in Kings Cross- I was hungry... He told me that we did not have the time, and opted for another, a well-known pub-and-restaurant outfit instead. We went, I ordered a burger, and I must say I was disappointed. I could have cooked a better burger at home.

If the product is bad, then it doesn't matter if your marketing is great. No amount of advertising I see from that pub is going to want me to go and eat from them again. Maybe, yeah, I will go for a drink.

One of the biggest mistakes I made early in my career was to focus too much on the tools – the Facebook adverts, the Google Adverts, the creation of a great content marketing strategy. I toiled to create a great brief for the design to be perfect, and to be sure I sent newsletters at the right time. But the most important aspect of marketing is the product. I did not spend time understanding the product, and how it makes people's life easier. I spent a lot of time on the tactics and not on the product. I believe I made this mistake because I was focused on the external – on how it looks and not how it works.

A few years later, I understood that the product is the most important aspect. How can we improve the product? How can we add a feature and improve our customer experience, so people talk about our product with their friends? Here's an example. We worked with a massage therapy studio and I recommended to the owners that they enhance their waiting area – add something unique that people will love and talk about. They added three types of interesting teas; the first tea was a 'relaxing' tea, the second was a 're-energise' tea, and the third tea was an 'invigorating' tea. They asked each client how they wanted to feel, and when the client told them they gave them the appropriate tea.

Somebody might have had a very bad day, and gone to the massage therapy studio because they had heard about it from a friend or saw something online. They decided to do something about their bad day. The reason why that customer came in might be because of word of mouth, or because they saw their content or read their story. That is marketing. For me, marketing is about driving a positive change. It's about inspiring and influencing people to choose the better version, to find a better way to solve their problems, to make them feel good about themselves. Marketing for me is about being a *bridge* towards a certain road the customer wants to go. It's influencing the other person to take the right action for them.

Marketing goes beyond advertising, email marketing, social advertising, posting on social media or taking pictures. A lot of people think that marketing is advertising. It is not. People market their TV shows, their podcasts, their books, their profiles on Tinder, their pets on social media. Marketing is the change we want to make.

I met a gentleman once, the way we all meet random gentlemen in this city. No, no, I mean met him at an event, I asked him what he did for a living, and he told me that he does 'marketing'. I asked him what does he do *exactly*, and he said 'I run ads'. There is your problem, right there – marketers think they 'do marketing' by running ads.

One of my favourite authors, Seth Godin, explains in his book *This Is Marketing*:

> *"Marketing does matter. Because marketers make change happen. That's the work. Not to run ads, not sell crap, not to invent hoopla. Marketing makes change happen. If you're not proud of the change you're making, do something else. It turns out that showing up with the right work for the right people in the right way is a powerful tool in making change happen.*

I truly believe that marketing is all about making a positive change happen, and one of the reasons I lost my passion is because I lost the meaning of it all. What was the point of me getting another client? More money? Okay, that's awesome. More team members? Okay, that's awesome. I didn't see a positive change happen. I worked with people that didn't want to make a difference - they wanted to make profits but didn't look at the impact they were making.

Then it hit me and I realized we need to change this. People are thirsty for more stories, they want a better quality of life, and they can be inspired - so why not be a bridge to those people?

In the hospitality industry, most hotels' marketing consists of selling rooms with online travel agents (OTAs). That's not marketing, that's *lazy* marketing. Hotels have an opportunity to change people's lives for the better, to make their life easier, to educate them, to teach them something new, to make them feel at home.

And, please, no, I don't mean your 'home away from home'. I really don't understand how so many hotels use this tagline. It's like a tagline from the 1980s, yet is still used by so many hotels. I don't want to stay at home when I'm away, funnily enough, I want to experience something different.

In the fitness industry, most gyms are promoting their classes and their properties, showing us how great their gym is or how great their class is. They can be so much more than that. They can inspire people to look after themselves, they can inspire people to go after their goals, their dreams, their aspirations, they can inspire people to become better humans.

Like anything in life, we can use something to make a positive change, or we can use something to destroy things. We can make a decision and say to some clients, 'This is not for you, this will not work'. We can choose to find great clients, and teach them why we care about this particular problem and why we are solving this particular problem.

A business is here to help us solve a problem. If we are not solving problems, then, perhaps, we shouldn't be in business.

Great marketing can help us reach more people and impact more lives. Great marketing can inspire people to take action for causes that matter, causes that we are passionate about. Great marketing can help us unite. Great marketing can make people smile, laugh, and make this world a better place.

Throughout this book we will be talking about how we can use great marketing and create more purpose driven brands. My goal with this book is to be of service to you. In some way, like the most diligent waiter. I will be sharing ideas to help you cross the bridges you need to, and reach your destination.

Chapter 2

What is a Purpose Driven Brand?

There are different opinions about what a purpose driven brand is. Some people think it's a marketing gimmick or trick, or something you say to increase your sales. There is some truth in this. Some companies do use it as a tool to increase sales, but it does not last. It never actually manifests into something meaningful because the year after that purpose they find a new purpose, and then a new one after that, because the 'new purpose' is meant to increase their quarterly sales. It's like anything in life really, are all lawyers honest? No. Do all accountants have the right values? No, of course not. The same applies to women that say 'all men are dishonest'. There are nearly 67 million people living in the United Kingdom and 49% of them are men, have you met all the men in the country? Have you met all men around the world? No, of course not. Not all men are dishonest. The same applies to marketers; not all marketers are liars.

What do I mean when I say purpose? What does it actually mean? Have you ever met someone who is passionate about piano? Have you ever watched a movie called *The Pianist*? It's a biographical drama produced and directed by Roman Polanski, based by the memoir The Pianist (1946), written by the Polish-Jewish pianist and composer Władysław Szpilman, a Holocaust survivor. The pianist, Adrein, goes through hell, but when he plays the piano, he plays from his soul, he is passionate about the piano. You can see it, you can feel it, you can understand it even if you don't have sound or subtitles. He had a purpose; he was dedicated to his craft, the piano.

At a conference I attended a couple of years ago I overheard a conversation between a young guy sitting behind me and the event speaker, Grant Cardone. From their conversation it became apparent that the young guy was famous in his arena. He was an artist. I didn't know exactly who he was until last week. I stumbled across an advert on Instagram from Stephen Ridley, a pianist and musical artist in the UK. The advert was about learning piano. I went into the rabbit hole of looking at his Instagram account and listening to his work. The guy is so freaking talented, it's amazing! And you can see it in his eyes, in his voice, in his demeanour. I followed him on Instagram, and this is rare – I don't normally follow celebrities or artists. But the reason

What is a Purpose Driven Brand?

I followed him is because his passion for piano is inspiring. I don't know the guy, but I do know that he is very dedicated to his craft. He definitely has a purpose. What I'm saying is that we can sense someone's purpose, and its merit, and that purpose garners admiration, even when we can't quite name that purpose, or describe it adequately - perhaps even when we are not in the same field. Even without being able to describe it, or know what it is, it still matters and inspires us.

A few months ago, Netflix released *The Last Dance*, a ten-part documentary. The documentary was about Michael Jordan and other players of his era. I was never a basketball fan, and I never followed Michael Jordan, but after watching the documentary I was inspired by his work ethic. We look at high profile people and think, 'Yes, they worked hard', but we don't understand how hard they work. To Michael Jordan's fans, he is 'MJ'. Regardless of the struggle that MJ endured, he overcame those struggles. He was driven by his purpose; if he didn't have a strong purpose he would not have kept going.

One of the favourite speeches is from Steve Jobs, and it is about purpose. He spoke at Stanford Commencement Address in 2005. Here is an excerpt:

'I was lucky, I found what I love to do early in life. Wozz and I started Apple in my parents'

garage when I was 20. We worked hard and in 10 years Apple had grown from two in the garage into a two-billion-dollar company with over 4,000 employees....

Sometimes life is going to hit you in the head with a brick. Don't lose faith. I'm convinced that the only thing that kept me going was that I loved what I did. You've got to find what you love and that is true for your work as it is for your lovers. Your work is going to fill a large part of your life and the only way to be truly satisfied is to do what you believe is great work. And the only way to do great work is to love what you do. If you haven't found it yet, keep looking and don't settle. As with all matters of the heart you will know when you find it and like any great relationship it gets better and better as the years roll on. Keep looking, don't settle.'

We can see that Steve Jobs had a purpose. Even when he got fired from Apple he kept on going, went on to create Next, and then he came back to Apple and completely revolutionized how we use technology today.

What is fascinating is that Apple today doesn't just have clients, they have fans. That love comes from the

What is a Purpose Driven Brand?

vision that Apple had. I will talk about their story in the following chapter, but coming back to Steve Jobs - he worked hard to improve the product because he loved what he did, because he had a purpose. Even today, after he is gone, look at Apple in comparison to any other company, and consider how simple their products are, look at how beautiful the experience is. This is because one man had a purpose that inspired others, including Jony Ive, Apple's previous chief design officer – and it is, of course, design, that is central to Apple's success.

The reason we see people go through adversity and come out on the other side is because they have a strong purpose. They had a strong WHY. When we don't have that WHY it's really hard to maintain hope and motivation.

There are a lot of companies that start out because the founder saw a problem in the market and wanted to solve that problem by innovating a product or a service. Usually, the founder struggled himself with a problem and decided to take things into his own hands and created a solution. He wasn't focused on creating money, but instead on finding a solution, and then figuring a way to sell and promote that solutions to potential clients.

I'm not talking about big organisations that create new products every week just for the sake of meeting sales targets. I'm talking about companies that care about what they do, and the majority of these companies are small companies. There is another type of company as well, one that looks for a gap in the market and finds it. But their ultimate goal is to sell the company to tech giants for millions. I'm not talking about brands that are driven in this way.

What I'm talking about is brands that truly believe in what they are doing and see themselves as part of the solution to a bigger problem. These brands are not for everybody, and they don't offer the cheapest products. You see them innovating, creating new solutions, improving, to a degree that you might say they are obsessed.

If I say people prefer to buy from purpose driven brands you might say, 'Alex, says who?' Well, let's look at some data. Not stories, not beliefs, but *data* about how consumers behave.

Accenture research (From Me to We: The Rise of the Purpose-Led Brand) shows that nearly two-thirds (63%) of surveyed global consumers prefer to purchase products and services from companies that stand for a purpose that reflects their own values and beliefs, and will avoid companies that don't. The other fascinating fact is that 62% of consumers want companies to take a stand on the social, cultural, environmental and political issues that they care about the most.

As in every case, it's not everybody. It is easy to assume that 'all' people have the same beliefs and the same habits. No, of course not. Some people pay millions to buy a house, or thousands to buy a Tesla, and then shop at Lidl Supermarket. I should know – I've met them!

But there are consumers who are drawn to brands committed to using good quality ingredients. And more than you might think: 76% of those in Accenture's study said that they prefer to buy from a company that has good quality ingredients.

Another 62% said that they are focused on reducing plastics and improving the environment, and 65% are concerned how the company treats their employees.

Research from Cone/Porter Novelli (2018 Cone/Porter Novelli Purpose Study) suggests that 80% of consumers say that when they buy a product from a purpose driven company, they feel they are playing a part in making a positive impact. It makes sense, because people want to be part of the solution, they want to be part of something bigger than themselves, we all believe in different things and causes. I have to apologize for saying 'we all'. Not everybody; some people on this planet, because, you know, you have a guy like Johnny who lives for himself.

People who believe that a company stands for something will keep buying from that company. This is where loyalty comes in. Cone/Porter Novelli reports that nearly 8 out of 10 (79%) of people in America say they are more loyal to purpose-driven brands than traditional brands and 73% are more willing to defend them.

Today we must also contend with social media, where everything that a company is saying or promoting will be defiantly criticised - or admired. We can't hide from the fact that everybody has a voice today; customers use social media to voice their dissent, and to call out unethical behaviour, and this reflects extremely badly on the companies named. For companies of all sizes, it affects the bottom line; in larger companies it affects their share price, too.

We all know that social media is effective if done right. Two-thirds of consumers told the Accenture study that they think their protest actions - including boycotting brands or calling them out on social media - can make a massive difference on how the company behaves. 36% reported being disappointed by how a company acted, which betrayed their belief in what the company stands for. Nearly half (47%) stopped doing business with a company in response to a moment of brand disappointment. This is what happens when brands don't truly believe in what they stand for.

The hashtag #MakeAmazonPay trended on Twitter in December 2020; it was approaching Black Friday, and people planned to boycott Amazon for not paying taxes, treating employees poorly, and other things they claim Amazon is doing. Social media has power and can damage companies' profits.

Historically, brands usually stayed neutral on hot issues, but there is a growing research that inaction on current political and social causes is proving increasingly alienating to consumers.

Why not put a LGBTQ+ flag outside your store and say you support the LGBTQ+ community and keep your bottom line growing? Because just sharing an opinion on a topic or issue will not do the job. What is needed is a meaningful commitment to causes that the company's core audience cares about.

Following the violent death of George Floyd in 2020, you saw a lot of brands hurry into an association with the #BlackLivesMatter campaign. My question is, why didn't they jump on this campaign at an earlier point? Why they didn't do anything against racism the year before?

Why is it that we see so many companies jump on different topics when everybody is talking about them, yet when nobody talks about them, they don't? If you believe in something, you speak about it when nobody else is. You won't be stopped because it's not 'trendy', or it's not cool.

The goal should be to find something that the company truly believes in and go in whole-heartedly - not just a little bit, and not because it's trending.

The cause that the company chooses should be at the core of what the brand is doing, this way the brand can differentiate itself. You might be thinking about a cause to choose, or how do you communicate that, well we will cover this in the later stage in the book - in Chapter 6, I will share with you the five steps you can follow to find your purpose and how you can articulate it and promote it.

Research by Kantar Consulting, a world-leading data, insight and consulting company, found that brands with a high sense of purpose experienced a brand valuation increase of 175% in the past 12 years, compared to the median growth rate of 86%. We have the data that shows us people prefer to buy from purpose driven brands. But there is a more important element – the most important element, I believe – and it can't be found in data. It's fulfilment. We want to do things that fulfil us.

The waiters at the restaurant works every single day to save money to buy a new microphone to sing because she loves it; the delivery driver delivers parcels all day to come home at night and work on his comedy; the woman in office that comes home after work and works on her new candles because she wants to 'light up' the world, the guy who is an accountant by day comes home to work on his guitar skills. Humans around the world want to feel fulfilment - it's a feeling

What is a Purpose Driven Brand?

we have when we love something that we do and we want to learn and excel at it. It's the feeling you have when there is a deep sense of tiredness from working all day, but when you turn to that project your soul wakes up, your eyes light up. It's an energy, it's an invisible energy and we all know that it's there, because we have felt it, and we feel it when somebody starts talking about 'our' topic. We want to be part of that. Fulfilment is an interesting concept because when we are fulfilled, we are willing to sacrifice, we are willing to go above and beyond. Like the pianist I follow, his energy through his work inspires people around the world. It's magical, in a way.

Today we can fly across the globe because two men, The Wright Brothers, believed in something bigger than themselves. Sir Douglas Bader flew in the Royal Air Force during the Second World War, and fought for Britain so we can have freedom today. Nancy Johnson invented the ice cream maker before freezers were even invented in 1843. The reason we have fire escapes today is because of a pioneering woman, Anna Connelly, in New York City – in 1887, she invented an external metal staircase. One of my favourite games, Monopoly, was invented by Elizabeth Magie. Originally designed to demonstrate the evils of unchecked capitalism, Magie's 'The Landlord's Game' was patented in 1904, 30 years before a man patented a very similar game called Monopoly and sold it to Parker Brothers. The reason why we have coffee filters today is thanks to Melitta Benz. Despite what her name may suggest, she was not Italian; she was a German entrepreneur who invented an easy, minimalistic way to make coffee by placing it in a filter and pouring water over it.

The reason why we have Wi-Fi today is because of a lady called Hedy Lamarr. She was a WW2 movie star who created a frequency-hopping communication system that would guide torpedoes without being detected. Her ground-breaking work paved the way for the modern invention of Wi-Fi, GPS and Bluetooth.

We have an opportunity to stand up for something, and we need to, more than ever. We need people like you to stand up and say 'Let's make change happen', because we've had enough. We can stand up, not because of fame, or money, but because we might make this world just a little better.

Chapter 3

What is Storytelling?

I think that we have the word 'storytelling' confused. I believe that a lot of people, especially marketers, throw the word 'storytelling' everywhere because it sounds complicated, and when something sounds complicated, it's easier to charge more for that complicated thing. I see and hear phrases like this all the time:

> 'We do great storytelling; let's do email marketing.'
> 'We do great storytelling; let's do a photoshoot.'
> 'We do great storytelling; let's do Facebook ads.'
> 'We do great storytelling; let's do content.'
> 'We do great storytelling; let's do an article.'
> 'We do great storytelling; let's do a cookbook.'
> 'We do great storytelling; let's post on Instagram.'

With this (mistaken) mindset, everything is a story. Me going to the toilet is a story if you look at it this way. But a story is not a sentence or couple of sentences that are created to communicate something. Some might argue that 'everything is a story' – well that is not true, not everything is a story. Or you might say something that has a beginning and an end, no, that's not a story either. Let's look at the examples below and see if we can call each a story:

An article
A joke
A movie
A game
A conversation
An advert
A video

What is your definition of story? What do you consider a story? Think about that for a minute or two.

Is a book about how to make poetry a story? Perhaps a tutorial on YouTube is a story. Maybe a TED Talk is a story?

If we go back and look at storytelling, we will see that we have told, used and relied upon aural stories for over 100,000 years. Written communication began only 6,000 to 7,000 years ago.

If we understand how the internal structure of story works, we control the message. We have the ability to learn and make sure that our brand story is perceived how we want it to be perceived rather than others making up their own stories about it.

Somebody told me that 'Everything is a story' – this is not true. How on earth is this remotely true? Everything is not a story, our daily life is not a story. Most of our conversations and gossips are not a story. Story is not the information, it's not the content that we communicate. A story is a way of structuring information, a system of information elements that most effectively create the essential context and relevance that will engage the receiver of that story and enhance memory.

I became obsessed with answering the question, 'What is a story?' I asked people what they thought a story was. I watched videos on YouTube, I watched documentaries on storytelling, and I read a lot of books about storytelling. What was interesting is that different people answered the question differently, they perceived a story in a different way.

Some people say that stories create an emotional connection, and I myself used to say that, because a great story has the potential to create an emotional connection.

Creating a story does not equate to creating an emotional connection; it only has the *potential* to. I didn't always make this distinction clear, but I'm doing it now. Some people say that stories make people cry. Some say they involve the reader and make things more memorable; some say that they make people feel a certain way. These are all desired outcomes of what stories can do - it's how the author or the creator wants the other human on the other side to feel – but it does not mean that this is what all stories do. Some stories are so boring that you actually stop reading, watching or listening to that story in the middle. It is a feeling of frustration. You know the kind of story, the one a mate in the pub started telling us a story a year ago, and still hasn't finished? Yeah, those type of stories. The kind where somebody is telling us what happened to him last week at work, or how somebody in the company was having an affair. There is a difference between stories we want to listen to and those…we don't.

Even authors and practitioners of narratology don't define a story in the same way. They all have different views and opinions about what a story is. But what we can do is look at the core basics of a story. Every single story has a structure that you can actually see. Joe Franklin (1986) a Pulitzer Prize winner, said that 'Just as all uniquely individual human beings have brains, hearts, stomachs, and pancreases, all stories have a common set of attributes that are arranged in a certain, specific way.'

The very core of a story is about overcoming adversity. There is usually some conflict presented. If adversity or conflict is not present there is no drama. By drama, I mean there is no action. People can't relate to something that has no emotional journey. And if there is no drama or emotional journey, it will not hold anyone's attention.

The biggest challenge I face when creating a story and speaking with business owners is the conflict aspect. Most business owners and marketers want to be seen as perfect, but a great story must have conflict, and conflict can be an obstacle. Ideally, we want to recognise the adversity that the company has faced, ideally we want to own that adversity. You know, people talk about authenticity but when it comes down to it and actually *being* authentic they shy away. The more authentic and honest we are about flaws and shortcomings, the more people will relate and love our brand.

A very simple example is to compare Eminem's fans to those of Lil Wayne. Eminem is known to have some of the most loyal and dedicated fans, do you know why? Eminem in his songs talks about the struggle. In *8 Mile*, in a famous scene - the rap battle with Papa Doc - he goes on stage and literally freestyles every single negative thing that his opponent, Papa Doc, might have on him. He tells us that he is white, he lives with his mum in a trailer, he's got a dumb friend Cheddar Bob who shot himself in his leg with his own gun, and so on. In his songs he talks about the struggle, the pain. He is vulnerable and authentic. Lil Wayne on the other hand talks about money, success, women, lots of women – all the shallow, superficial things, right? There is no struggle in his songs. I believe this is the reason why Eminem has the most loyal fans in the world. The key here is to understand that being authentic and vulnerable requires a lot of strength.

I started my agency, wow boutique agency, in 2010. I slowly started working with different clients, won numerous awards, then hired more people and slowly grew to a small company. Over the years, we've worked with more than 80 brands and created more than 500 projects. I travel and do speaking engagements at events and universities.

That – just four sentences – is it a story? Here is another example:

I was fired in November 2010 from an advertising agency. I had bills to pay, and rent to pay, so I was scared for my future. I didn't know what to do, so I started focusing on my 'side hustle', helping customers with their online marketing. I always believed that there is a better tomorrow, that there is a better way to do things, even when everything was dark around me. I got lucky at some point and got more clients on board. I was knocking on every single door. I'm honoured to have worked with some beautiful and talented people in the agency, who taught me so much. We managed to work with more than 80 brands and created more than 500 projects, and even win a couple of awards down the road. Our goal is not getting awards or getting more clients, our goal is to make things better, our goal is to always find a better way, we want to help our customers empower their customers. We are on a mission to create a better tomorrow so that our communities can thrive and grow.

Which of the two examples feels somehow more satisfying, and more relatable? I'm willing to bet it is the second one. The goal shouldn't be focused on showing how great we are, the goal is to be authentic and human. People relate to a journey with ups and downs, they related to struggles, and ultimately overcoming those struggles. A small note here; those struggles should not be small, immaterial difficulties. Think of life. Life is all about overcoming struggles and adversities. Living purposefully means we face challenges and we overcome those challenges.

Stories are not statements about the company. This is really important. Most companies have statements on their 'About Us' page online. It is usually an ego-boosting statement that makes the company look good and doesn't help the customer decide or understand something about the company. This type of selling and marketing is called product-focused. We want to move away from product-focused selling and focus on purpose-focused selling.

We as human beings are eager for stories, not data, not lectures, not dissertations, not essays, not boring presentations, not ego boosting 'About us' pages, not adverts, but interesting stories. I don't see people turning to Netflix for advertising, or say they can't wait to listen to another boring presentation.

Last year, I was chairing an event. When you chair an event, you introduce the speakers. But it's not just introducing them; it's also listening to their presentation so you can comment at the end and follow up with questions. When the event was finished, I was relieved - I said to myself 'Never again!' Because the speakers bored me so much. They were presenting numbers and statements about their company, and how great they were, and how they offer this solution and that solution.

The power and effectiveness of stories come from specific informational elements that form the core architecture of stories, this matches what we humans need to see in order to turn words into meaning.

A story is not the medium: it's the tool that we use to distribute words. It is the structure. Story is a system of elements creating context and relevance to engage receivers, and enhance memory and the creation of meaning.

Every effective story needs to have motives and goals. Our actions have no meaning without these

What is Storytelling?

two very important components. That's why when we create a story we need to really think and communicate about our motives. Here are a few examples:

- I went downstairs and opened the fridge.
- The lady went into a supermarket.
- The man ran to the bank.

Our brain will Immediately create assumptions about the three examples above: he went downstairs and opened the fridge because he was hungry; the lady went into the supermarket to do some shopping for home; the man was running because he needed money. We assume things. Our brain doesn't like it when we don't know things, hence we make an assumption.

- I went downstairs and opened the fridge because I heard it was beeping, and water running.
- The lady went into a supermarket because she was going to complain about the bread she bought that morning.
- The man was running to the bank because he was going to rob the bank.

A goal creates relevance and meaning for the action we or the character takes.

A story needs to have conflict and struggle. It's so important yet so many companies miss these important elements. Conflict is energy, it creates tension. Conflict is what drives excitement in a story.

Here's an example.

Maria wanted a burger. She went downstairs and cooked one. The end.

This is so wrong on so many levels. It's not worth telling, it's not worth listening to and such a story is offensive to some people. It simply violates some core tenet of narrative structure.

Here's another example.

George wanted to start a company. In 1980 he opened his company. He grew his company to 30 team members. Today his company offers the highest quality products in the market. The end.

Do you see similarities? It's practically the same. There is no tension, there is no structure and yet the majority of companies that's how they communicate.

We want it to be hard for Maria. We want her to struggle to get the burger. We don't want Maria to have a ready-made burger for her. We want her to face some risk while going downstairs, we want her to struggle making that burger, we want her to cry when she finishes cooking that burger. The reason we want her to struggle is because we will find meaning and value through her struggle.

We couldn't care less about Maria, or the burger until there is struggle! Struggle is what unlocks the key to a successful story structure. A lot of companies want to communicate their achievements but it's the struggle to get those achievements and accomplishments that will give meaning, relevance and value to the other person reading about it.

So is a story sentences with struggle? No. It would be easier if we could separate the word story to avoid confusion. Unfortunately, we can't. This is what a story really means:

A story is a detailed, character-based narration of how a character struggles to overcome an obstacle and reach a very important goal.

Now let's compare this to the dictionary's definition: 'A narrative account of a real or imagined event or events'. The dictionary focuses on event an is this plot based. Stories have a character and are driven by details that describe character's goals, obstacles, struggles and motives. The struggle and the goal gives the reader a reason to keep on reading, it keeps our brains engaged as we need to know what will happen, we need to know if Maria will struggle for that burger.

A fantastic example is when I was doing a brand story for a client recently, I was in the process of interviewing different people from the management. When I interviewed the founder, he shared with me the story of how he started the company back in 1989. The process of creating a brand story requires to have conversations with the founder(s), ask the right questions to find out what their beliefs are and find their why. He shared with me some really inspiring stories; how he was sleeping only a few hours a day to keep his company, how he didn't know anybody in the industry and introduced another service in his company so he could get some other clients in order to survive, how his wife told him that her water broke and they needed to go to the hospital to give birth while he was serving a customer and wanted to finish the order first. From these stories you can see an underlying theme, a belief that the man had. He had to overcome so many struggles and he did, even until recently, how their company responded to COVID-19 crisis as well. Yet on their website they only had their victories, how successful they are.

With a great story you can inspire change. But a great story can also be used to manipulate others.

What is Storytelling?

Some examples of how companies manipulate: they post aspirational messages implying that our life is not that great, and only if we buy this product will it improve, or, of course, peer pressure. The most overused variety of peer pressure must be 'Sarah just bought this'. Other manipulative stories they might create include reducing price (scarcity), and ideas based on fear. I think the worst tactics are used by OTAs - you are thinking of booking a hotel room, you go to booking.com and it looks like the whole world is trying to book that same room that same weekend. No wonder people get anxious!

We always have a choice about what we do, and how we use what we learn. It's like having a hammer – one can build a house, or tear it down.

The beauty of a great story is that we don't need to compete on price, or use manipulative tricks to make people buy our stuff. Instead, we can make positive change happen.

In a later chapter we are going to talk about how we can create a *brand story*, the core message of a brand. We will create a story that your potential clients will be engaged with and remember. Your brand story will help you create an emotional connection with your customers, it will help you give a story to your customers that they will be able to relate to and share it with their friends and family.

Once we have a story, we will create a slogan. It's the last element that we will create because the slogan should represent the whole story, it should summarize your purpose. Your slogan should be used everywhere, it should be on all your marketing collateral. But more about it in the later chapter.

Chapter 4

Focus on the Purpose

One of the biggest problems I see business owners make is that they focus solely on the product, on what they are selling. A fitness coach focuses on how great his classes are; a hotel focuses on how fantastic their rooms are; a service provider focuses on how many years of experience he has; a vegan restaurant focuses on how delicious the food is.

There are many factors in play when we humans buy. It's not only because something has a specific feature or benefit; it's not purely because of cost or location. While some aspects are more important than others, at times, humans don't make buying decisions for one reason alone. A potential guest looking to book a hotel room might say that location is the most important aspect, but if he finds a boutique hotel that requires him to walk an extra 10 minutes he might choose that hotel. When I booked a hotel in Amsterdam for a speaking gig, I booked a hotel that was not near to the venue I was speaking at. Why? I wanted to experience that particular hotel. Some say that people make decisions purely on price. I have to disagree. If price was all that mattered, we would have two types of cars, and two brands of underwear. This is not the case. We buy things based on emotion and we use logic to justify what we bought.

The first step is to truly understand that it's not about the product, and it's not about you, the owner - it's about the customer. Here's the hard part: we need to remove our ego. This is the hard part, because the ego is something that we can't physically see and yet it's there on a preconscious and conscious level. In *The Chimp Paradox* by Steve Peters, the author describes an inner chimp, an irrational and impulsive being that inhabits our minds and constantly is looking at himself. Sigmund Freud's three states of Id, Ego and Super Ego is similar to this. There is a little voice that goes in our head that reminds us, 'But I worked so hard to achieve this', 'I worked day and night to win these awards', and on it goes.

A lot of companies declare that they have quality products and services, but when we compare their communications to their designs, there is an unhappy disparity - they say they have quality product but their marketing collateral, and its design, doesn't reflect the quality of the product. The goal is not to say that we have quality products or services, but for people to say that themselves. When you look at brilliantly designed packaging without trying the product you can *feel* that this product is a quality product. When you look at a product with poor packaging, you are in doubt.

Even if the quality of the product or service is exceptional, we as humans don't believe it. We might have the 'best' candles in the world, but if you, the seller, say it, people are sceptical. They won't really believe it until they see it for themselves. The same applies, whether it is products or services. You might meet a designer and she might say that she is the 'best' designer in the world, but you will not believe her until you see her work, right? The same applies when somebody has the word 'expert' in their title: we immediately become a little bit hesitant about their expertise. Self-proclaimed experts are everywhere.

The 'best' is subjective, but we can all agree when something is high quality. I might claim that I'm a great chef but once I cook something for you, you will discover the truth! That's where self-awareness comes in, and being aware of what the market tells you. By 'the market', I don't mean mass market, I mean the desired audience you want to sell your product or service to. That's why we need to prove that we know what we are doing. There are different ways that we can prove that we know what we are talking about, or that our products are high quality, before the customer buys anything. Before the customer decides to buy something they make assumptions about the quality and the value of the product based on design, packaging, and tone of voice.

The second step is understanding there is a huge difference between what we believe in and what we do. Let me elaborate the difference between believing in something and doing something. Every single company knows what it does, what it sells, we all know what we do for a living. I create brand stories; I do content marketing; I'm a hairdresser; I sell food; I am in finance and accounting. This is what we do.

But what is exciting for people to learn is what you stand for, what you believe in. This is how we can differentiate ourselves from the rest: we can communicate what we believe in and stand for. It's basically writing down your values and communicating them in an appealing way. The 'what' we do is just proof of what we believe in. We all know that talk is cheap, but actions speak louder than words. In our case, when building a brand story we need our words to be loud and interesting, and when somebody experiences our product they can confirm that what we say it's true. Once we have our values and actions aligned, we don't have to compete on price, because, let's admit it, competing on price is a race to the bottom.

Focus on the Purpose

Why did we get obsessed with the competition and what others are doing? I believe it comes from a mentality of capitalism at all costs. Most of the time in larger companies, the conversation is about how to reduce costs, how we can find cheaper ingredients in China, how we can maximize productivity from our team, how we can increase the number of parcels a delivery driver can deliver in 59 minutes and 59 seconds.

A lot of time is wasted on looking at what the competition is doing, how they are doing it and other details that focus on maximizing profitability. The reason this mentality developed is because when the Industrial Revolution was born, from about 1760 to sometime between 1820 and 1840, companies realised they could mass produce goods. People, as we know, didn't have all the options we have today, buying 'stuff' and 'clothes' wasn't a thing. So, factories had a problem – they could create huge production, but they needed to sell the products that they created - they needed people to spend their money on products. Slowly, people were introduced to shopping. In order for companies to grow, create more jobs, build more churches and houses they needed people to spend their money on things. Then investors got involved, and they needed to get their investments back. So that's why we as society started to push growth. We need to grow, so we can grow more. Don't get me wrong, capitalism is a great thing, I'm not against it, I love capitalism, but I think we need to be mindful about the 'growth at all costs' mentality.

It doesn't have to be that way. What happens when the competition is wrong? What happens when the competition doesn't know what they are doing, or are copying somebody else? When we obsess with the competition, we forget to pause and think about what makes us unique. We forget what makes us valuable.

Rather than competing, we need to remember – perhaps rediscover - the reason we started the business in the first place. When we communicate what we stand for, it comes from a place that is genuine and authentic. It comes from a place of understanding and loving. We stand up for what we believe, we truly believe in it, and we don't need to copy anybody. And the best part about this is that nobody can copy our passion, nobody can copy our energy, and nobody can copy our belief.

People can follow our belief and, ideally, us, because they believe in the same thing. Why do you think some companies have loyal clients? Think about that. Is it because they were the cheapest? No, I don't think so. Why are you loyal to certain brands?

Actually, when I ask this question 'Why are you loyal to certain brands?' or 'What is your favourite brand? a lot of people respond by saying they don't have a favourite brand, and yet after two minutes of conversation with them they start telling me 'Oh, I always go to Clarks', or 'I always travel with British Airways', and I laugh because we make so many decisions that we don't even think about on a conscious level. Different people care about different things: it's impossible to care about everything and every category.

Great companies have a common pattern; and by great companies I don't just mean the big ones, the huge corporations that are on the stock market and are doing billions in revenue. By great companies I mean and include small companies, solopreneurs, an ambitious single mother that lives in East London and grew her business slowly by caring about her customers, the two relatives that are running a factory and making shoes, the two brothers that run a small hotel and know their regulars by their name when they check in.

If we want to truly win, we need to focus on mattering to our customers. And how do you suggest we matter? Well, it's actually pretty simple. The owners that build these companies know what they stand for; they don't need to tell us that they are 'passionate about what they do' because we can see it in their eyes when they talk about their industry and the change they are trying to make. What they stand for is proven by their actions, what they believe in can be seen in their products and services, what they do is visible. Their story is the same regardless of trends happening in the market.

Have you ever met a person that started talking about a topic you couldn't care less about? Let's say you meet a person that loves squirrels. You might be like me, you don't really know much about them. Whenever I look at one squirrel, I love it, I always smile because they are so cute and funny in a way, but I don't actually know a lot about them. But the person that you meet starts talking about them with excitement, he tells you how intelligent they are. He tells you how squirrels collect and store nuts so they have food to last them throughout winter, and that this helps trees, because they forget about where they put their nuts - grey squirrels bury nuts all over the place and they forget about them, resulting in trees growing in new areas. More than half of the trees we see are planted by squirrels that forget, can you imagine? When this person talks to you about it, you start caring more about the topic because he cares so much about it. You start to know more, and care just a little more about the topic.

When somebody actually cares about a topic, they make us care as well. They say passion is contagious, well, it really is. Have you ever got inspired by an accountant telling you what they do and what they stand for? Nah, I don't think so. I'm sorry, accountants, but you know that it's true. Most of the times when you meet an accountant the conversation is the same. But can you imagine meeting an accountant that communicated and articulated what they stood for? He would stand up and start communicating not about accounting, but about the cause he is excited about.

Here is a very important element that we need to distinguish – there is a difference between what we stand for and what we do. What we stand for is a cause, it's a cause that is bigger than ourselves. The cause could be wanting to help stop animal cruelty, and what we do is a bridge towards that. For example, Unity Diner, a vegan restaurant in East London, opened in 2018 with the mission to make a positive difference (it is owned by activist and educator Earthling Ed). Their mission is to contribute towards creating a more compassionate future for all animals. All their profits go towards animal rights campaigning work and their ultimate goal is creating an animal sanctuary. In late 2020, they achieved their goal and bought 18 acres of land in the rural Midlands of England. Their mission is to offer a place for animals where they would never, ever fear being exploited, abused, or killed.

The cause could be more specific. I may want to reduce the number of abandoned dogs in the UK, or it could be that I want to help people make a mental connection between animal welfare and food. There is a huge lack of education and awareness about animal agriculture, with too much meat and dairy industry marketing designed to make consumers forget about the animal.

What you stand for needs to be linked to what you do and why you chose that cause. Yesterday I saw a hotel share on Instagram that for the month of December they are supporting Street Smart, a charity that helps the homeless, and are asking their guests to add £1 or more to their booking. This is a great initiative - but why? Why is this hotel supporting this cause? Perhaps the hotel thought it's a great cause and they wanted to stand for something, but, personally, I receive it as a marketing gimmick. I think what they are trying to do, is create a perception in people's minds that they are doing an altruistic activity. They want people to tell a story that might be like this; 'Look at them, look how great they are, helping homeless people.' Next month they might be supporting the bees, because that happens to be trending. You see, I don't really believe in what they are doing because the brand, that particular hotel, has never communicated it before.

This is the biggest problem I see with brands that are saying that they support certain causes. Today they support LGBTQ+, tomorrow is something else. There is no depth in what they support, and it shows. It's like when we hear a billionaire donated millions to a charity – but we don't know why they are doing it. I would love to see or hear them say why they are passionate about specific cause.

There is a charity called Charity: Water, founded by Scott Harrison. This charity has mobilised over one million dollars around the world to fund over 59,000 water projects in 29 countries, projects that will serve more than 11 million people. What's interesting (for me) is 'Why?' Harrison was indulging himself in nightclubs for a decade. He declared spiritual, moral and emotional bankruptcy. He then spent two years on a hospital ship off the coast of Liberia, saw the effects of dirty water first-hand, and went back to New York City on a mission. There is a story you can judge for yourself.

Danny and Amy Buck started honu, a sustainable e-commerce company selling jewellery. They also want to save sea turtles. From what I understand, they were on holiday in Hawaii when Amy encountered a beautiful species of turtle; this was the inspiration for honu. They learned that six out seven species of sea turtles are endangered and they wanted to prevent their extinction. They've since partnered with Sea Turtle Conservancy in Florida, and donate 10% of honu profits to aid their amazing work. They have a more meaningful purpose than the hotel mentioned above.

One of my favourite examples of a vision shared is Martin Luther King's I Have A Dream speech. He said 'I have a dream that my four little children will one day live in a nation where they will not be judged by the colour of their skin, but by the content of their character'.

People believed him, they shared the same vision as him, and they felt connected with him. It wasn't the 'I have a plan' speech, or the 'I'm the best speaker' speech. It was a cause that was higher than himself. This is a great example of how our mentality should be when we create a story.

Pause for a minute and let us do an exercise. Write in a notebook or on a notepad this sentence, 'What change do I want to see in the world I live in?' Write in detail five things that you would like to see happen in the next five years. With those things written down, write an action plan on how you can be part of that change. We can't spell 'activism' without 'act'.

Chapter 5

Why Your Brain Loves Great Stories

> *"We are, as a species, addicted to story. Even when the body goes to sleep, the mind stays up all night, telling itself stories."*
> — *Jonathan Gottschall, The Storytelling Animal: How Stories Make Us Human*

When I was in school, I was a very bad student. Science was my least favourite subject, and I don't even remember going to a biology class. Back then, if you had said that years down the line I would be immersed in reading about science, I would have laughed. But here we are, diving a bit deeper into science. The reason I turned to science is because I wanted to learn how a story affects our brain, how it affects our behaviour and our buying decisions.

I recently connected on LinkedIn with a gentleman called Lennert De Jong, chief commercial officer at Dutch hotel group citizenM. When I first saw his profile subtitle, it did not include his job title, or how he spent his time. It just said, *'Without data, you are just another person with an opinion.'*

I loved that. The quote, attributed in the first instance to the statistician W Edwards Deming, stuck in my head because it's so true. You might have one opinion and a friend of yours might have another opinion, but they are just opinions, informed by experience, how we view the world and what we see. We can argue about opinions all day long. Science, however, is much more difficult to argue with.

A gentleman walks in, wearing a tuxedo. He walks to the bar with confidence, orders a martini, and briefly looks around the room. A gorgeous woman approaches him, introduces herself and asks for his name. He is a very 'hard to get' man, you know, the alpha male type as society calls it. He has had many liaisons with members of the opposite sex but never commits. He rarely makes long-lasting relationships with women (or men). He turns to the woman and says 'My name is Bond, James Bond.'

After watching the Bond movies, men go out and buy products - products they saw in the movie. We want to buy that Rolex, to feel like we are James Bond, and you definitely need that Tom Ford tailored suit, because you always wanted a Tom Ford suit, right? The Barbour jacket that the secret agent wore in *Skyfall* immediately sold out in all stores after the movie was released in cinemas. It's described as 'The Bond Effect'. The retail price for those jackets was £400, and when they sold out at the retailers, people started selling the same jacket on eBay for £2,000.

Heineken paid £28 million for the privilege of seeing Bond sip from a green bottle in an early scene of the movie. This covered almost a third of the film's estimated £94 million production budget. That's a very expensive sip, don't you think?

The most successful businesses understand that they need to invest in a well-constructed narrative. Science is putting a much finer point on how stories don't just sell more products, they change our attitudes, beliefs, and human behaviour. Neuroscience and brain scans show us how a story can change activity in our brains.

Vincent du Vigneaud, an American biochemist discovered a neurochemical called oxytocin: it's a signal that communicates to our brain that it's okay and safe to approach others. Oxytocin is produced when we are trusted or shown kindness, and it inspires us to cooperate with others. It does it by enhancing the sense of empathy, our ability to be able to experience another's emotions. Empathy is very important because it allows us to understand how other people are feeling.

Paul J. Zak is the founding director of the Centre for Neuroeconomics, and author of *Trust Factor: The*

Science of Creating High-Performance Companies. He and his team tested if narratives shot on video would cause the brain to make oxytocin. They took blood draws before and after they showed the narrative, and found that character-driven stories do consistently cause oxytocin synthesis. The amount of oxytocin released by the brain predicted how much people were willing to help others.

To motivate others to help, a story needs to sustain attention, a scarce resource in the brain. To maintain this scarce resource, we need to have tension in the narrative. If the story includes tension, then that tension will be transferred to the viewer. If there is no tension, no stakes, then it gets boring and the viewer's attention will wander. To make sure that the person keeps on reading and consuming our content we need to include tension. When people consistently engage with the brand then they feel more emotionally connected, and when somebody is emotionally connected, they are willing to help that cause or brand.

Stories help us connect to the past and express often-universal beliefs. Without stories we would struggle to connect with one another. Can you imagine meeting a human being and the only words came out of his mind where what he does, where he lives and other statements? Oh wait, that actually happens on a daily basis - a lot of brands communicate like this, and a lot of strangers at networking events communicate exactly like this.

It's estimated that as much as 65 percent of all human interactions take the form of social storytelling, which means gossip. And if there is a story included, then there is great potential for empathy and exploring.

Listening to or reading a story activates the auditory cortex of the brain, and fires up your left temporal cortex – this is the place in our brain that is receptive to language. This part of the brain is also capable of filtering out 'noise', meaning the clichés we use. Once you are engaged in a story, other parts of the brain also start to participate.

When we feel an emotional engagement with a story it is because the frontal and parietal cortices have been stimulated. (The parietal cortex is located near the centre of the brain, it's behind the frontal lobe and above the temporal lobe. The parietal lobe contains an area known as the primary sensory area.) Activity in the frontal and parietal cortices is when the brain 'gets excited' in a way. When we read a powerful description of food it stirs your sensory cortex, while descriptions of motion or action will get a response from the central sulcus - the primary sensory motor region of your brain. For example, even just thinking about running can activate the neurons associated with the actual run.

When we read or hear good stories, they stick longer with us; sometimes days, sometimes years. Great stories make us remember an event or an important information about a specific topic. As Jennifer Aaker, professor of marketing at Stanford Graduate School of Business, writes, "People remember information when it is weaved into narratives up to 22 times more than facts alone".

There is a difference between someone telling you a story about how to survive and someone sharing a fact. I can say, 'There's an animal near that tree, don't go there' or I can say 'My cousin was eaten by a malicious, scary creature that lurks around that tree, don't go over there'. The second story is more effective, you most probably will not go over there, unless you like taking extraordinary risks.

When we listen or watch to stories our brain is working, so our mental activity brings changes in our body. If there is tension - we are watching a scene with Bruce Wills from *Die Hard* - our stress hormone cortisol is released into our bloodstream, which leads to greater immersion and responsiveness to the arc of a story.

That's why it's important to be aware and intentional when building our brand story. If we want to bond and increase trust, we need oxytocin to play a part. When we listen to a story that is interesting, we become more human and we bond with the other person, we create more empathy, and we connect with other person. This will enable trust and it's an important component in marketing, especially when we are selling a product or a service. Without trust, no transaction can happen.

Before the lockdowns to contain Covid-19, I went to comedy clubs every Sunday because, well, I love comedy. What I actually love, and what we as humans love, is when our body releases endorphins. When we have a higher level of endorphins, we are more creative and relaxed. Endorphins are not just released going to comedy clubs: exercise has the same effect. That's why I think I got addicted to my HIIT (high-intensity interval) classes and running! Endorphins are released when we give as well – when we donate, volunteer or help others feel good. The US-based National Institutes of Health found that people who gave money to a charity activated pleasures centres in their brain. Yoga and meditation are also well known for increasing endorphins.

There is a 'happy chemical' as well, it's called serotonin. Some people call it a 'happy chemical' because it contributes to our wellbeing and happiness. Serotonin helps us regulate our mood naturally, and low levels of serotonin are linked to depression. When serotonin levels are at a normal level, we should feel more focused, emotionally stable, happier and calmer.

Last but not least is dopamine. I feel like dopamine is the fun kid that everyone wants to have at their party. We all know that dopamine is associated with pleasure. But it's not just pleasure; dopamine causes humans to feel something that will help them be focused, remember things, and be motivated. To create dopamine, we need to include an interesting question, a controversial statement, cliff-hanger or a plot twist. A lot of comedians use plot twists. Dopamine is mentioned a lot when we look at how we respond, at a physical level, to notifications on our smartphones – this is what happens when we receive likes and shares on social media. It plays a part in why you see so many people glued with their phones all the time. But it's not just social media; it's associated with any kind of pleasure.

We talked about all the 'good' chemicals, but what about some of the more dangerous ones? Say hello to cortisol and adrenaline. Hello darkness, my friend. Think of cortisol as a built-in alarm system for humans. It's when we are in crisis this chemical enables fight-or-flight response.

Adrenaline is a fight or flight chemical. It's when you jump out of a plane with a parachute you have what they call an adrenaline rush. (Actually, I got addicted to this one as well. I'm scared of heights, can't stand them, and decided to go skydiving. I went and jumped twice, and now one of my goals is to get a skydiving license – and, therefore, more adrenaline in my body.)

The thing is, when we are selling something, cortisol and adrenaline can work against us. Adrenaline works on a very physical level, increasing heart rate, increasing body blood pressure, expanding the air passage of the lungs, enlarging the pupil in the eye, redistributing blood to the muscles, altering the body's metabolism, and more.

Mentally, both cortisol and adrenaline spur the following: feelings of intolerance, irritability, a lack of creativity, memory impairment and poor decision-making. Cortisol is actually a very important chemical, designed to command the brain's attention. It communicates to our brain that it needs to stop and pay attention to that particular thing because it can learn something. So it is important in storytelling. But it must be used in small doses - too much cortisol and the audience will feel uncomfortable and 'switch off'.

To start writing a brand story, we need to understand the importance of each chemical and be intentional about the result we want to create. We need to look at each sentence and paragraph to make sure what is included and what kind of chemical you want to release. In the following chapters I will share a framework that you will be able to use to create your own brand story.

You might not be a scientist, or even care about science, but we all can look at scientific proof to understand the importance of a great story. I'm not a scientist and I don't think I will ever be, but, certainly, I have to look at science and make sure that I learn and use what science teaches me. We can see from science that our brains love great stories. There is scientific proof that great stories are at the core of humans, our society and culture was built because we were able to communicate and create stories. It's up to us as storytellers to use stories to make this world a better place.

Chapter 6

Building Your Brand Story (The 5 What's Framework)

To build a brand story, a lot of deep questions need to be answered. You need to go back and look at the past and see what inspired you, what made you tingle. If you are a business owner or a freelancer, it all started with you. If you are a team member then you will need to have honest and have in-depth conversations with the founder of the company.

At way boutique agency, we usually take a lot of time to create a brand story. Just this week, I spent two days at the hotel we are working with to create their brand story. I interviewed team members, and management, too, in an effort to understand what they believe in, what drives them, what inspires them, what do they fear, what change do they want to see in their community and why they work there.

A brand story is the foundation of your brand. Your potential customers, clients will be able to read and understand what you stand for. A great story should really be 'about them' not 'about you' because it's all about them. Once you have your story on your 'About Us' page you will need to incorporate it in all your marketing collateral. Your slogan will come out of this story, and it needs to be everywhere, promoting your story.

There are a couple of phases you need to go through. The first phase is total immersion in the brand, understanding the culture, the mentality, the goals, ambitions, the fears, the unspoken desires. This is the development phase, where you immerse yourself with the brand, with the customers you want to serve. Think of it as the foundation of the brand. Think of it as building a house, you don't start with the interior design you start with the foundation.

Each step is imperative as it will set the tone for your brand story and your tagline. When creating your brand story you shouldn't think that it needs to 'sound nice' for marketing, you should aim to make it feel right for you, the owner. You can polish the words you use in the last stage and play with them but as the foundation, you need to make sure it's something that truly relates to you and represents you, as a brand and as a team.

Once you have the story ready then you can promote your story on your website, on your social media, you can create a video, incorporate your brand story in your social media strategy. Your story should help you with your content marketing strategy, it should navigate you through marketing campaigns you want to create.

I have created a structure to help you create an effective brand story.

I call it 'The 5 What's' – the five elements that each story must absolutely have.

1. WHAT DO YOU BELIEVE IN?

The story should start with what you believe in. What is the main cause that you are working on? When somebody asks you what you do, you should respond with what you believe in, rather than what you do. When we communicate and say what we do - all the logic, like facts and figures – it doesn't drive behaviour. 'Oh, you've been an accountant for 10 years. Nice.' There is nothing here for me. I might be looking for an accountant but you *sound* like all the other accountants. You can't take that statement and keep a conversation going unless accounting happens to be your passion which in most cases it is not. When we communicate with logic, we communicate to the left-hand side of the brain – the logical side of the brain. We want to communicate to the right-hand side of the brain, the emotional part of the brain, where memory and creativity is, the part of the brain that connects with the heart.

A great example is how author and business consultant Mike Michalowicz turned his career from being an accountant to helping entrepreneurs. One of his books is *Profit First: Transform Your Business from a Cash-Eating Monster to a Money-Making Machine*. I adopted his methodology by opening five bank accounts (Money In, Tax Account, Owners Pay, Profit, Operational Expenses) and it helps me tremendously. I do not like accounting, I'm not a huge fan of numbers, but I still bought the book, read the book, and implemented the lessons. Mike doesn't talk about accounting; he talks about entrepreneurship, and making entrepreneurship simple. He believes in simplicity. Guess what? I believe in simplicity, as well. Most accountants talk about numbers, yet this man talks about simplicity to get you to buy his book and then do your numbers!

When you start with WHAT you believe in, and WHAT you stand for, you capture the other person's attention.

Here's an example of how an accountant could communicate:

> *'I believe in simplicity, you know. Life is so beautiful and I think we complicate life too much. I want to make everything simpler, so we can enjoy the beauty of life.'*

This statement makes you want to hear more. You are intrigued, and if you believe in the same thing (simplicity) you will have more to talk about. Rather than talking about numbers and tax returns.

Start your story with what you believe in.

2. WHAT PROBLEM DO YOU SOLVE?

You need to tell people about the problem you are solving – and the problem needs to be from the customer's perspective, not that of your business. The customer doesn't care about *your* problems, they care about their own problems. It's important to understand what consumer problem you are solving and communicate that.

We need to position ourselves as a bridge for the client, not the hero. Most companies position themselves as heroes and focus on solving their business problems. The customer doesn't care if hoteliers pay a high commission to OTAs and lose out on that revenue; the customer cares about safety, how clean the place is, the cancellation policy and other aspects of the hotel.

If you were an accountant, you might say something like 'Do you know how much time we need to spend doing our taxes, VAT and all the other paperwork? And how hard it is to find someone you can trust with your finances?' This is an example of how you can look at a problem from the customer's perspective.

Every business solves a problem, but we have to remind ourselves that it's the customer's problem that we are solving. The problem should be very clear: once the customer reads or hears the problem they should relate and think 'Yes, I do have this problem.' If the customer doesn't relate it means either it is the wrong customer, or the problem is not relatable.

A challenge you might face here is that your company solves many problems for different customers, and you would want to include them all, but you can't, because it will confuse the customer. You might have different customers; a lot of businesses do. Young Millennials and perhaps Generation Xers, for example. You will need to choose one main problem, for the most important clients you want to acquire. It doesn't mean you will turn down others, it means you are focusing on this type of customer. Then you can create other 'sub-campaigns' or landing pages for other audiences. But for the main brand story, you need to choose one problem. If you choose more problems it will confuse the customer and you will lose him. We need to include one main problem, one big problem in our brand story.

3. WHAT IS THE OBSTACLE TO OVERCOME?

In every story, the main character needs to overcome an obstacle. We can call it the villain in the story. You can make a person the villain, or another company - for example, you might see a problem with the industry and you might say that a certain kind of business is driving this sort of behaviour, and it is not benefiting people. So you are not naming one company as a villain, only stating some companies that do this type of thing, and you don't agree with it.

The obstacle needs to be hard to overcome; if it's too easy, people will get bored. It's like anything in life, if you have a challenge, but it is too easy, you lose interest.

It might be that the obstacle is internal – to overcome a limiting self-belief, for example. I am currently training for a 100KM ultra run from London to Brighton. The obstacle I have to overcome is internal and physical – I've never done run more than 20KM in my life and I don't know how to train for it. This is an example of an obstacle a potential customer who is getting ready to run an ultra-marathon might have.

Another example is that I'm currently working on is for a hotel campaign. The problem is that people have been stuck at home in service of others (helping slow the spread of Covid-19), and at a cost to themselves (increased stress and loss of peace of mind). The tension is that they are taking care of others first, instead of taking care of themselves. At a later stage, we will introduce the solution to capture the sale; they can renew themselves with nature at their footsteps without harming others.

We need to be very clear about the problem we want to solve so the consumer will relate with us.

4. WHAT IS THE SOLUTION?

This is where the solution comes in. If I want to get fit for example, I need to go to a gym, or a HIIT studio, or get a personal trainer. To complete that 100KM ultra run, I may need a very good running coach to create a training program for me, running clothes, and a suitable running watch. In this part, you need to think of it as the solution in your industry; it is not about you, specifically. You need to be positioned as the bridge to help our customer, the hero, achieve their goal. Position the solution as the bridge.

I wish I understood this concept much earlier in my career. For many years I positioned myself and the agency as the hero – this was a mistake, which cost me a lot in lost opportunities. Don't make the same mistake I did. You need to position yourself as a bridge.

People have goals and aspirations, we all do. Different solutions solve different problems hence help us achieve our goals. Think of it this way: you want to drive to a destination, and in order to drive to that destination you need to cross different bridges. You might need to cross the Tower Bridge to achieve on goal, then you might need to walk through Millennium Bridge, you might need to cross Southwark Bridge or any bridge. If you think of your solution as a bridge it will help you position yourself better.

This is not a place for any statements about your product or your amazing services – these things are not interesting in this particular moment, and they are not a story, just someone's opinion about something.

Think of heroes in movies. If they could solve their own problems, they would never get into trouble. In every movie you will notice that there is somebody else who is helping the hero. Every single human sees themselves as a hero in their own life. It doesn't matter how altruistic, kind, selfless the person is, the world still revolves around them. When a company unknowingly positions themselves as 'the hero', the potential customer subconsciously switches off because they don't want to compete with the company; in their subconscious minds they just want somebody to help them. That's why it's important to position ourselves as bridges.

5. WHAT DO YOU DO?

This is where you communicate your product and your services. What do you actually do, how does your product or service will help people achieve their goals? I believe this part is what most people communicate. Everything needs to be connected so it ends nicely with what you do. When you describe what you do you need to use active words, colourful words to paint a picture that will stick in your customer heads. This is where you can add your awards or some important data that you want to mention, but it's very important that you don't overdo this. You don't go from 'I'm an accountant' to 'I've been an accountant for 10 years now, I started since 2010, earned two degrees, have a hundred testimonials and ramble on'. It needs to sound and feel like it's a genuine person that cares about what they do and are truly immersed in what they do.

A very important factor to think of is that you never, ever include your prices in your story. If you include price in your story then it's game over. A person needs to be sold on the idea first before looking at the price. So many times, we see salespeople focus on the price before we are sold on the concept yet. The price doesn't really matter when I have not been sold on the product, or that particular idea is not going to help me achieve my goals.

With this framework, you can work on creating a meaningful brand story. If the story is done right it will connect you with the right people. It should open their eyes, evoke an emotion, create an interest, it should move them in a way.

Building Your Brand Story (The 5 What's Framework)

There is a formula that giant companies use and it's available to all of us - it's available to the small independent hotel down the road and it's available to the yoga instructor who wants to inspire more people to take yoga classes. The best way to see it is to reverse engineer a story. When I was learning to create briefs, one of the exercises was to reverse engineer advertising campaigns and understand the consumer insight and the problem the ad was trying to solve.

It seems every business book includes an Apple case study, and there is a reason why. I have had the pleasure of meeting Ken Segall, author of *Insanely Simple*. He is the guy that worked with Steve Jobs on creating the Think Different campaign and the iMac. When we had a chat, one of the things that truly made an impression on me is what he said about how to stand out and succeed. In order to stand out and succeed, he said, you need to remove all the clutter, all the noise, and keep one thing - make it really simple for people to understand. Think of the majority of communications and adverts. They always look cluttered – decision makers say the following: add our message, add our website, add our phone number, add this, make the logo bigger, a bit bigger, more and more. It becomes cluttered and noisy, and the consumer gets lost.

Let's look at the *Think Different* campaign. Apple didn't position themselves as heroes, no, they positioned themselves as the bridge. This is what their campaign said:

> "Here's to the crazy ones.
> The misfits.
> The rebels.
> The troublemakers.
> The round pegs in the square holes.
> The ones who see things differently.
> They're not fond of rules. And they have no respect for the status quo.
> You can quote them, disagree with them, glorify or vilify them.
> About the only thing you can't do is ignore them. Because they change things.
> They push the human race forward.
> While some may see them as the crazy ones, we see genius.
> Because the people who are crazy enough to think they can change the world, are the ones who do."

Can you see in their 'story' that they don't mention the product, they don't mention that they are the 'hero' of the story? Well, what they are saying is that they admire this type of people. And when we say that we admire a certain type of a person it says a lot about us, about our beliefs and our identity.

So Apple positioned itself by saying that people with passion can change the world. In that campaign, they included 17 iconic personalities: Albert Einstein, Bob Dylan, Martin Luther King Jr., Richard Branson, John Lennon (with Yoko Ono), Buckminster Fuller, Thomas Edison, Muhammad Ali, Ted Turner, Maria Callas, Mahatma Gandhi, Amelia Earhart, Alfred Hitchcock, Martha Graham, Jim Henson (with Kermit the Frog), Frank Lloyd Wright, and Pablo Picasso. Apple understood the power of storytelling, and became a company that cares about the customer.

In 1983 Apple launched a computer called Lisa. It was the last project Steve Jobs worked on before he was let go. The ad for Lisa was a nine-page ad in the New York Times mentioning all the computer's technical features. It was all about logic, it was all about the technical aspects. It failed. Of course, it did. When Steve Jobs came back after running Pixar, Apple launched a new advert in the New York Times with two words: Think Different.

The story is not about Apple, the story is about the customer. They are not the hero, they are the 'bridge' for people with passion. They play a role akin to Q in the James Bond movies. You are the hero when you buy and use Apple products. You might say that Apple is not 'the best computer company in the world', but it doesn't matter. Whether they are the best or not, people don't buy the best products. Instead, they buy products from brands that they care about.

Now, there is a key difference between you and Apple – you will build a story that is meaningful, purposeful to *you*. This is really important to comprehend, we need to create a brand story that will touch some people's hearts. We shouldn't think about what celebrity we can get, or if we should use outdoor advertising, or how we can target the masses - this is mass marketing mentality, and we are not into mass marketing mentality. We want to focus on fewer people that will care about our purpose as we do. We can find people like us, people that care about the same thing. But in order for those people to connect with us emotionally, they need to hear and listen to our story.

Once you create your brand story using this framework, I can guarantee to you that people will start caring and connection on an emotional level with your brand. It will give you an opportunity to humanise your brand and create loyal customers.

CHAPTER **7**

Stop Talking About the Product

If you look at how advertising was done in 1950s and 1960s, you will notice a common approach: it is always about the product, how the product you are looking at is the greatest product of all time. The focus is on the company, brand, and product.

In the UK, the first television advertising was broadcasted on 22 September 1955, on the newly established Independent Television (ITV, as we know it now). The first radio commercial was not broadcast until 1973. When big brands realised that they could use mass media to advertise their product, they went all out. But back then we only had a few TV and radio stations, all relatively new, and so people actually listened to ads - they were effective.

What followed was relentless expansion: in 1960, the UK had two television channels: BBC and ITV; in 1983, there were four channels to choose from, in 2020, we have over 480 channels. That's not including Netflix and other on demand platforms like Disney Plus, Apple

TV and others. Media companies, advertising, social media, newspapers, and outdoor ads all compete for our attention.

There is evidence our attention span is decreasing. In 2000, Microsoft conducted a study measuring how long people could focus on one thing for a specific amount of time. The results showed that the average person's attention span was 12 seconds. A later Microsoft study, conducted in 2015, showed it had dropped to 8 seconds. A study from the Technical University of Denmark suggests that our collective global attention span is narrowing because of the abundance of information we have at our fingertips.

As business owners and marketers, we believe that *our* advert and our piece of content is so important that the audience is sure to stay and consume it. The reason why we think so it's because of cognitive bias. Our human brain is powerful and it's always looking for shortcuts. Cognitive biases are a result of our brain's attempt to make things simple to digest. How we perceive different things are different, we might remember some aspects of an event and we might remember the things we want to remember so we go with a particular narrative. It's easier to spot cognitive bias in others rather than ourselves – but we all have it.

Well, our advert and our content it's important for us, it's not important for them: people have hectic

Stop Talking About the Product

lifestyles, tough schedules, and the last thing they want is to waste time consuming adverts.

Commerce Signals estimates that 40% of all media spend is wasted – a number that come out from about 60 different studies, said Tom Noyes. Now let us have a look at the cash. In the UK, advertising spend was forecast to reach £23.6 billion by 2020.

A couple of years ago, I was fortunate to hear Dave Trott speaking at a conference in Twickenham Stadium. Dave is a creative director and author. He said something so powerful it has stuck with me since. He said that roughly £17 billion pounds was wasted in a single year of advertising - because no one notices ads. That number, £17 billion, was based on the total ad spend in one year, 2007*. This is how people remembered the ads they saw:

4% was remembered favourably.
7% was remembered negatively.
89% wasn't remembered at all.

If we speak with marketers and media creatives, most will say that their ad was 'remembered favourably'- but we know it's not true. Trott saw that roughly £17 billion was wasted on advertising because people don't remember it at all.

We can't please every potential customer, and we don't need to. Today, we have an amazing array of options for creating content for the right people. We have blogs, podcasts, videos, ebooks, newsletters, and many other ways of creating content and engaging with our customers. But when I speak with marketers and business owners about creating content, I hear very often that they don't know what to post on social media; they don't know what type of content to create. They are lost, because they think 'What else can I say about my product?' They are thinking of product-first content. The solution is to not to talk about your product or service.

How many times can a hotel's Instagram page post a picture of the same bed, at different angles? It is dull. There are brands that I use, I pay money for their products, but I unfollowed them because I find their content boring. Don't get me wrong, there are hundreds and millions of people that might be following that account and they get value from it. I might be different because I see it in a different way, and I'm very mindful about what type of content I consume on social media.

How many times can you post the same food pictures from a restaurant account? I know there are a lot of 'foodies' out there, some of whom will diligently 'like' all the pizza pictures on Instagram, but what kind of impact does this make? Surely, it does help – to a degree. But how many people remember what they liked on social media 24 hours after? Not a lot, I guess.

The same applies to other industries, hair salons, for example – it's the same. Fitness studios, the same, nearly all of them follow a common pattern; post about what you sell. And I understand, it's engrained in us and in a way it makes sense.

How can we add more value? Think about media companies, influencers, and comedians. What do they have in common? Media companies think of the consumer first – what they can create and post on blogs and on social media to engage with their audience. Influencers think of how can they get attention and build a following so people trust them, like them, and ultimately buy from them. Comedians create content to entertain their audience and be top of mind.

But Alex, what about selling our products? We are a company, at the end of the day. Yes, I hear you. Companies that are growing exponentially and have a following on social media, or a large number of newsletter subscribers, are value focused, and customer focused, and their content reflects that. I believe that if we want to be relevant as companies, as brands we need to become media companies. The question needs to be 'How can I create content that adds value to my current and potential customers?'

We do not need to talk about the product. We need to create content that will educate, inspire or entertain them. How do you do that? Well, let's say you need content for your website blog, social media, newsletter and podcast. You will need to think of your main objective for each channel. What do you want people to do on Instagram? What do you want people to feel about your brand on TikTok? You can write down topics that you will talk about. The topics you choose depends on your story. What does your story include? What are the problems you are solving and how do you want to change our society for the better? Is it mental health? Is it animal rights? Wellbeing? Lack of education? Corruption? Inequality? Finances? Climate change? Obesity? Addiction? Healthy habits? Self-care? Suicide help for men? Preconceived ideas about how things should be? Domestic violence? Racism? The list is endless.

There are so many things that we struggle with as a society, and we could improve in so many areas. Society is created by every one of us, each individual. Just yesterday I was running on Euston Road, and opposite Warren Street Station there was an advert with the following message 'abusers work from home' – highly relevant during the government-imposed lockdowns of 2020. I'm genuinely shocked that today, in this day and age, we have men abusing women. Yet I don't see a lot of brands standing up for these issues.

It's important that your content and your story aligns with your business. As an example, we can use a fitness studio. Most fitness studios focus on the 'product', and focus on getting people to sign up to their gym or their studio. We have gyms that charge £9 per month, we have gyms that are open 24 hours. If we have a look at 100 studios and gyms in the UK, we will notice a common pattern – most are focused on the 'product'. Their content on Instagram is all about how great their studio is. But what would happen if they focused on the other aspects such as creating content to help people develop a new habit? There are plenty of books about habits, there is plenty of research about how we can create a new habit and ditch an old habit. One great book is *Atomic Habits* by James Clear, in which he talks about how we can create new habits. A fitness studio could work with a professional in the industry and do live Q&As on social media. They could collaborate with mental health professionals and create content to help people overcome challenges. They could create content to help people overcome depression.

In 2017 I quit smoking. If I'm addicted to something now, it's running. There are a lot of reasons why I quit smoking which are common sense; health is the main reason. One of the reasons I run is because I read an article from Jim Kwik, a renowned brain coach. He recommended in that article how to switch habits, from bad to good. The main reason I quit smoking was because of Allen Carr's book *Easy Way To Stop Smoking*. I read it a couple of times. I also watched documentaries about how cigarettes are created and the history of smoking. So you can see I changed my life because of the content I sought out, and the things I read. That is how important good quality content is.

Another topic the fitness industry can talk about is food. They can talk about how we should eat, how to overcome binge eating habits, how to stop eating junk food, the sociology behind our food addiction, why should we fast and so many more questions they could answer. I would love to read an article about fasting.

A gym or a fitness studio could set a tough fitness challenge for their clients, and create a campaign around that. I recently completed a challenge called #75HARD which entails exercising twice a day (a 45-minute session each time, workout has to be outside), no alcohol, no cheat meals, 4.5 litres of water and reading 10 pages of non-fiction – all tasks must be completed every single day. This challenge wasn't created by a fitness studio but by Andy Frisella, an entrepreneur and podcast host.

There are just so many opportunities out there and yet we see everybody copying each other. We see all these models on social media, and these are not realistic comparisons for an average Joe. We all understand why they hire great looking models, male and female, but the problem with that is that once you walk in that studio, you don't see them, you see your friend Joe, and your neighbour Diana, who is not a supermodel but a normal woman. It doesn't inspire community, it doesn't inspire us to take action, it doesn't set realistic goals. If a gym could focus on being authentic – I know it's a trendy word, but I can't explain it otherwise – and showed us real faces, real people, then perhaps people would be reminded that a gym should be part of their real lives, too.

A fitness studio could stand up and say 'We want to end depression in the UK'. That's what they stand for, their gym or studio is a bridge to help people with depression. Or they could stand up and say 'We want to end obesity'. There are so many avenues to choose from, but it needs to be truly aligned with the brand. It needs to have a valid reason why it wants to solve that particular problem – perhaps because the owner suffered from depression, or the chosen topic. It needs to be connected.

It's obvious when somebody doesn't really believe in what they say. I was a leader at Run Talk Run, a mental health running club. The club concept is as it sounds – you run and talk, there is no judgement or competition. They have running leaders across the UK and the world – it's a great club and I highly recommend it. It's founded by Jess Robson, she is a fantastic human being and truly believes in what she does. Every week different groups meet at their own set locations where they start and finish the run.

Where I used to be, there was a yoga studio, we left our bags and changed clothes if we needed to. The yoga studio also supported the running club. One day I met with the studio founder and had a chat with him. I asked him why he supported Run Talk Run. I still don't know why. The answer was like 'Yeah, just because there are so many running clubs out there…' He gave me the impression that the main reason was his studio benefited from an association with a mental health running club. I used to go to that yoga studio. That was one reason I stopped. Later, looking at the studio's content, their website and what they stand for, it made sense – they don't stand for something, they are just a studio that wants clients, is trend-led, and will add anything to their website. This type of brand doesn't inspire you to do yoga. They don't inspire you to take action. I have free classes there and I don't even take them – and it's been a year.

Hotels have a problem: their occupancy rates have dropped dramatically. But they have another problem, the first one is they keep mentioning at every single conference: OTAs. They complain about how Booking.com, Expedia.com, Hotels.com and other online agents are taking their commission. Well, I'm not going to get into the conversation about direct bookings, but I will share some ideas that hotels can use to help regain a focus on what they can do.

If we look at the content of a hundred different hotels – Instagram content, to be more precise – we would see that most of them focus on the bed, free Wi-Fi, free breakfast and so on. What they could do is focus on the area around them, and create content that will help guests to travel with purpose. Help people understand why it's important to truly explore the city that they are visiting. Another content idea is sleep! Oh, how convenient, because their product is sleep, they are selling sleep. What I mean is, why don't they educate us about why sleep is so important? Why don't they educate us how we should focus on deep sleep, and REM sleep, and how drinking one glass of red wine is not good for our sleep. I'm not a sleep expert but Mathew Walker, author of *Why We Sleep; The New Science of Sleep and Dreams*, is (I recommend the book if you want to learn more). My point is, there is so much information out there. Hotels have the potential to speak about so many topics other than their breakfast. If a hotel wants to increase event bookings, they could consider creating content aimed at event organisers wanting to learn about selling more tickets for events.

Marriott hotels tripled their revenue through its content site Marriott Bonvoy Traveler (traveler.marriott.com). They create content that really connects with people and ultimately drives direct bookings. In 2018, Marriott Traveler attracted 3 million unique visitors, and increased visits to their individual hotel landing pages via Traveler by 80 percent. Revenue from hotel bookings is up 200% compared to 2017. What will you find on their website? You will find articles with titles like these – 'This Year, We Deserve To Be Pampered; Indulge in These Gift Ideas for Travelers', 'Judith Hill on Finding Hope, Roaming Where the Wind Takes Her and Fave LA Spots', 'How To Take Your Family's Remote Learning Plan on The Road'.

Some say 'We don't have the budget that Marriott does', or 'We can't build a studio like they did'. Oh, they built a studio? Yes, they built a studio to create short films. They actually created a short film, an action comedy following two hotel employees Christian and Gage. The roles were played by Hollywood stuntmen William Spencer (*Spiderman*) and Caine Sinclair (*How I Met Your Mother*). In the film they took down a gang of notorious art thieves. The film was shot entirely on location at the JW Marriott Los Angeles LA Live. The film sits at the intersection between branded content and pure entertainment. But we don't need to create a film like that, after all, we don't have the budget that they have.

Let us look at something local, something really small. A family-owned hotel called Central Hotel London, based in Kings Cross London, with 30 rooms, decided to work with amazing boutique agency called way! Yes, that's us. Anyway, I'm not bragging, but, look, we worked with them and we helped them increase their direct bookings on their website by 1500% within three months. We don't have the budget that Marriott has, and the turnover is definitely nowhere close to them, but we did increase their bookings using content that did not speak about the hotel. We used our story, our tagline, *'explore more, do more'* and we used creativity.

Another great example is Beauty Line. When we started work with Beauty Line, a leading beauty brand in Cyprus, we created a new blog, separate from their main website. It is called Beauty Diaries. The purpose of that blog is to inspire women with ideas, tips and thoughts about how they can enhance their make-up and personal style. The blog helps the brand with brand awareness, reach and the bottom line on their ecommerce website and their physical stores.

Another great example is from one of my favourite brands, Rituals. They are a luxury lifestyle brand who aim to transform everyday routines into more meaningful experiences. The Rituals concept combines home and body cosmetics with collections based on Eastern traditions. Every month I receive newsletters from them with interesting ideas about health and wellbeing. Their latest newsletter included an article on how we can have a mindful reset changing our brain. At the end of each newsletter, they always have a small banner that takes you to their ecommerce to shop. The goal of that newsletter is to inspire and educate – and if you want to buy a product you can. Some newsletters they send are sales newsletters – which I don't mind getting, because they mix it with value driven newsletters that I find interesting.

On the other side…. There is a brand that I think is fantastic – I use every day, I recommend them to my friends. This brand is Huel. You might not be familiar with the brand but they make nutritionally complete meal replacement drinks, and are one of the fastest growing brands in the UK. So, basically, I'm not cooking anymore but instead have Huel every day (except Sunday, when I do cook – but if we are honest, mostly I order take away). I find it amazing because I don't waste time in the kitchen and I can be healthy and save time. Now, having said that, I'm not a huge fan of their content, because they are very product focused. As an example, I received my parcel a couple of days ago and since then I received two email newsletters about the product. The problem here is that I'm not interested. Why? Because I've already bought the product – I'm a fan of the product, but there is no value for me in the newsletter. They tried to add a 'tip' on how to use Huel better, but at the end the call to action was 'Shop now'.

Their content mentality is product focused. Compared to Rituals, where they provide value *and* they sell, Huel currently doesn't really provide value (to me) in their newsletter or social content. If you are new to Huel, perhaps their Instagram might be helpful, but I've been buying from them for the past two years, and it gets a bit boring because I don't expect anything from them other than when they have a new product. What they could do is shift their mentality to adding more value.

Let's have a look at one of the best examples in not speaking about the product. Red Bull energy drink. Red Bull is often referred as 'The King Of Content Marketing'. If you don't know the brand and visit their website or their social media accounts for the first time you would think that they are a media company. Their whole website is a 'media' website where they have interviews with athletes, best music to train with, inspiration, how to content and they do have one tab where it takes you to their products. Even their website home slider has the following slides: out of 6 slides 5 of the slides are articles and stories, the last slide on their website is purely product based which says 'RedBull gives you wings' which coincidently the last slide.

You can see that the brand constantly is going above and beyond to create value with their content. Their mentality is putting their customers first and listening to them. No wonder they've become one of the most talked about brand of our generation. If you look at their content strategy they are always creating content about where their customers are going; music festivals, concerts, latest trends in skatepark, mountain biking, free-running in car parks and of course extreme sports. Red Bull's marketing strategy is not to sell the product, their ultimate goal is to sell the experience. This is something that any business of any size can do. It's something you and I can do and start doing today.

We can see a huge shift that is happening in the last decade from brands adopting the mentality of focusing on the experience, on not focusing on the product. There are many brands that are becoming 'media companies' instead of companies that sell 'products'. Volvo is another example. They created a documentary series on YouTube titled Human Made Stories; Defiant Pioneers which features 5 episodes that look into different human stories. You can watch the "Nemo Gardens" which is about a man in Italy building an underwater farm.

A fantastic example of a business that became a media company is Away. A company that sells suitcases has built a great brand through creating consistent inspiring content. They found a sweet spot between super-premium and inexpensive luggage to sell to customers using their own platform. Due to their growth, they've expanded from selling just suitcases to offering multiple bags, travel accessories and wellness products. Away has become a brand that people admire. How did they do that? By speaking about their products? No, by speaking about everything else but their products. They've become an 'Instagram Brand' with a following of 547 thousand followers.

Initially Away started out with an offline content strategy. The co-founders Steph Korey and Jen Rubio interviewed 40 people from the creative community, including a number of travel photographers and writers. This became a book called *The Places We Return To* – which became a sell-out. The book helped Away to exceed more than $12 million in first-year sales. This is a company that was created in 2016. This is not a company that has been around for decades.

They didn't stop just at creating a beautifully designed print and digital travel magazine, they created a podcast called "Airplane Mode" which helps people explore the reasons we travel and places we find ourselves.

Their content strategy is to create aspirational and engaging content that focuses mainly on lifestyle and the wider travel experience rather than their product. Their initial idea then evolved into a quarterly print magazine called *Here*. *Here* is now a stand-alone dedicated blog and quarterly magazine. In this they write about city guides, product recommendations, ideas, personal stories and other topics that give value to their reader. They even created a separate Instagram account for the magazine (@here.mag). A perfect example of succeeding by becoming a media company instead of a traditional brand.

The goal is not to speak about the product only, the goal is to mix your product with other topics. There are different types of content that you can use. Testimonials, for example. They are important, but if we post the same boring testimonials, people will not really believe it. If you create a content strategy that includes intentional and valuable things for your potential customers, they will consume it.

There is a way that you can say things. Say a girl, let's name her Sarah, goes on a date with Paul. He says to her:

> 'I'm making a lot of money, you know, Sarah. I work for a fintech company and I travel a lot, meet celebrities, eat at fancy restaurants regularly in Mayfair. I have worked with over a hundred clients, and get to hang out with wealthy individuals.'

I'm sure that Sarah will not go on a second date with him – unless this is the kind of man she wants!

What if Paul said the following?

'You know Sarah I wake up inspired every day because I'm doing something I really love. Sometimes it's challenging, yes, sometimes I do have bad days but when I get to help the end consumer manage their money it makes me feel alive. It gives me an opportunity to help others, like have a better way to save money, show people their spending habits with nicely designed graphs and give them the flexibility with a new type of bank. Personally, I grow every day as I learn from my team. I'm lucky to be working with hundreds of clients and I get to hang out with some great people – some of them well-known'

Do you think Sarah will go on a second date? I think so.

The way we communicate is in *what* we say and *how* we say it. I believe it starts with our intention. What is our intention?

There are times when we need to say that we worked with certain brands to increase trust, there are times that we need to mention that we have a certain number of years' experience, but the difference is *how* we say that. Like our dating example – the same message, delivered in different ways.

How we say things changes how the person reading or listening to us will interpret it. To create an emotional connection, to create empathy, we need to choose our words carefully.

Chapter 8

A Slogan, or an Ethos?

Once we have created a meaningful brand story, we need a slogan that represents it. A slogan is as important as the story, and if the slogan is not catchy or does not represent us, our story will be lost.

Think of it as a sentence that will intrigue people to look more into our story. Our story slogan should convey a clear message about what we stand for. It should inspire people to take action.

The first slogan that comes to mind is 'Just Do It' by Nike, right? It's so powerful, we use it in our daily conversation. We tell our friends to 'just do it' because it's easy, we all can remember it and it represents their story.

It is important that the slogan doesn't speak about the product. I see a lot of businesses with slogans communicating what they do, but that's forgettable and obvious.

A lot of slogans are, unfortunately, cheesy. They make you cringe. I understand from the business owner perspective that some of these may sound nice – because it's about their business – but from a customer's perspective it's not exciting. I admit there are some nice slogans that say what the company does in a subtle way, but I would avoid it.

Here are some examples of slogans:

Ted.com – Spread Ideas
Instagram – To capture and share the world's moments
Uber – Get there
Nike – Just Do It
Airbnb – Belong anywhere
Lego – Only the best is good enough
Apple – Think Different
Adidas – Impossible Is Nothing (Changed to "Adidas All In" in 2013)
Under Armour – The Only Way Is Through (2020)

Some people might call them mission statements. Indeed, a lot of marketers call slogans mission statements and mission statements slogans, but there are differences between a mission statement, a vision statement and a slogan. A marketing professor might tell you that a vision statement describes the long-term objective of a company, 'long-term' being 5-10 years or longer. A mission statement should be like a road map of how to achieve the goals you set in your vision statement; it defines the purpose of the business. It doesn't mean that is how companies use their mission statement. That's why I think the most effective way is to have a brand story, and one with the structure I recommend. You can have both, but, initially at least, I believe working on your brand story will be more effective.

A few examples of mission statements:

Starbucks – To inspire and nurture the human spirit – one person, one cup and one neighbourhood at a time
Nike – To bring inspiration and **innovation** to every athlete* in the world.
*If you have a body, you are an athlete.
Dove – We believe beauty should be a source of confidence, and not anxiety. That's why we are here to help women everywhere develop a positive relationship with the way they look, helping them raise their self-esteem and realize their full potential (vision statement)

Some companies have different slogans every year with every campaign – I don't think of these as company slogans, I think they are just campaign taglines. I believe the most effective way is to have one main slogan about your brand that represents your story, and if there are campaigns you want to run, use the tagline in those. The difference between a slogan and a tagline is that a slogan is something that should be as your permanent slogan – something that describes what you believe in, what you stand for, and a tagline is a campaign tagline that can be used to promote a specific product or service or a campaign.

Your slogan should prompt people to think about your purpose, the cause that you support. There are some great slogans out there, but there is no story behind them, there is no meaning. It's just a catchy slogan. That's why it's important to support your slogan with a story. A story will add meaning and depth to your brand.

What you stand for and what you do is in your story, and a slogan will articulate it concisely. At way boutique agency, when we work on a story, we turn to the slogan last, and play with words to describe our story. It needs to be as short as possible, and as clear as possible. It definitely does not speak directly about the product.

The goal is to get people to read your story: once they have, they will, ideally, connect with your brand on an emotional level, buy from you, and, ultimately, become loyal clients.

A Slogan, or an Ethos?

When somebody reads or listens to your story, they should be able to share it with their friends. Of course, not everybody is going to share and not everybody is going to like it, but those that do will become fans, loyal fans of your brand.

We often speak of and share examples of huge brands, and I think a lot of businesses are put off by that. You don't need to be a giant brand to have raving fans. We can see how small, niche businesses are thriving right now because they nurtured a small number of people who follow and love them. There is a huge cultural trend where people look for companies that support their causes. People want to join movements. Now is the time to focus and build a community.

When we worked with Central Hotel London, their tagline became *'explore more, do more'*. The goal of the tagline is to inspire guests to look up, to discover new places, and explore like a local, not like a tourist. When you truly explore a city, you get to see how locals live, you get to experience beautiful places and not be ripped off by touristy attractions. After our story, we must 'prove' that we believe in what we say by creating content that aligns with our story. We create content that helps current and prospective guests see what creative events are in the area. We don't just share pictures of the area, we include the history, or we tell the story of a particular event and the people behind it.

For example, we created content for the hotel's blog and social media accounts covering a partnership between the Kings Cross estate and talented creative Andy Leek, a three-month residency. The whole Kings Cross area was covered with positive messages in the hopes of bringing smiles – they spread a message of optimism and positivity.

People notice things that are different and new, but it's impossible for the human brain to pay attention to everything. Research done in 1970s estimated that we were exposed to 500 ads daily. That was before the social media era. In 2007, research from Yankelovich, a market research firm, showed that in England we were exposed to well in excess of 5,000 adverts a day; that includes social media, radio, newspapers, TV, trains, outdoor posters and all the other mediums. You might say you don't remember any ads, yet alone 5,000 ads. Well, this is the problem – you were exposed to 5,000 ads in a day, it doesn't mean you paid attention to all of them, most probably you paid attention to just one, if you did at all. Our brain can't absorb and digest so much information.

The only way our ancestors could survive in the jungle was to make a quick split-second decision. If you needed a day to decide if something was a friend or a foe, you would not live long. That's one of the reasons we have the ability to make quick decisions. We don't

A Slogan, or an Ethos?

have much time to tell people about ourselves – people make assumptions about a company, a customer service agent, a book, within seconds! And once we make a decision, we often stay with that decision, even when we are shown facts and data that it's the 'wrong' decision for us.

This is where your slogan can help you – if done right, it can grab the attention of your potential customer for a few more seconds and make them think.

You might say 'What about the product? If the product is good, people will speak about it without a story.' Yes, they will. An example is an artisan bakery here in Camden. Their products are delicious. Goodness gracious, their apple pie just melts in your mouth! I even bought the apple pie for a friend and told them about the bakery. 'An artisan bakery in Camden that makes delicious products,' is what I said. I didn't know what else to say about them, because I don't know anything about them and they definitely don't work on creating a brand story and giving their customers the tools needed. And of course, I don't have an emotional connection with them. If another artisan bakery opens down the road with a nice interior design and delicious food, I will go to that bakery and try them out. Do you see the difference? If I connected with them on an emotional level, if they had an interesting story, I wouldn't want to try other bakeries, and I would have something to tell my friends other than 'It is an artisan bakery.'

We start with a slogan to prompt our potential customers to read more about us, to learn more about us. A slogan shows that we are interesting and that we stand for something.

Chapter 9

Customer Loyalty Vs Brand Loyalty

I believe it's important to understand the difference between customer loyalty and brand loyalty. They are both important to a business to grow, but they are different. With a meaningful brand story you will not be able to create customer loyalty. Let me explain.

Let's start with customer loyalty. What does it mean? Customer loyalty means that a particular human is loyal to the company because it is convenient, they like the product, and the price is right. The customer usually is very satisfied with the company. Companies can encourage and improve customer loyalty by maintaining low prices and offering discounts – as we see a lot of companies do. These things convince people that the company they are using is one of the cheapest and most convenient for them.

Brand loyalty, on the other hand, is a different game. Brand loyalty is when a customer has an emotional connection with the brand. They identify with the brand on a personal level, there is a feeling about the brand. People who are brand loyal repeatedly buy from that brand because they know it will deliver on its promise, and they believe they have a 'special connection'. Brand loyalty may be conscious or unconscious, but pricing is not a big factor; customers simply feel that the brand is reliable and trustworthy, with a superior product.

The difference between the two is that customer loyalty revolves around customer spending; it is reliant on pricing, discounts, and savings. Brand loyalty is all about perception. Often when a customer is brand loyal he will have arguments and promote the brand to his inner circle. He or she becomes an ambassador. This doesn't necessarily mean that everybody becomes an 'ambassador' in the most obvious sense. Different people behave in different ways: some people are very quiet and will not be 'loud' about their purchases, and some people are proud and are 'loud' about their buying habits.

Brand loyalty means customers are more likely to try out other products from the same brand, whether they are more expensive or not. Customer loyalty means they will shop around if the company's prices go up, and if the company stops communicating (social, ads, newsletters etc). That's why we see year after year so many adverts from brands about their prices, about new deals and

Customer Loyalty Vs Brand Loyalty

special offers, because they know that they need to be top of mind.

I believe we all stand in different areas with different purchases we make. The reason why is because we all care about different things in life. Somebody who is health oriented, who values his health more, will pay more for a brand he associates with this same value system. You might care about technology and creativity, so you will invest more in a brand that is focused on those things.

Customer loyalty is much easier to gain: create special offer campaigns, lower your prices, and you are going to be playing that game. Unfortunately, this game is a race to the bottom. But this is what a lot of hotels do on OTAs – they play with pricing all day to win a customer.

If you observe how people sell you will see that one of the first things people say is it's 'a good price', or they will offer a discount before the customer is sold on the product.

Most companies are playing in this game, trying to gain new customers and increase their average ticket.

Brand loyalty is much harder to achieve because it takes time: the brand needs to stand for something. And it's hard work, quite frankly. A meaningful brand story will help you create more brand loyal clients.

But it doesn't stop at the brand story. Once you have the story, the foundation, you will need to execute the story and 'prove' this is what you believe. The ultimate goal is to create a deeper emotional connection with the customers. There are different strategies that you can use in the future to strengthen that connection, it's like a relationship, in a way. You have the foundation; you have the right customers and then you work on your relationship.

One of the biggest advantages with gaining brand loyal customers is that you don't actually need to spend money on advertising or content to convince them to come and buy from you. I will go as far as to say that you don't need to be constantly promoting to them. You *do* need to innovate – keep evolving and showing it with your packaging, communication, and other aspects – but brand loyal customers don't require so much effort to keep them.

The customer loyal buyer constantly needs to be reminded that you are there, that you are available, and your prices are the best prices. A lot of energy is spent on pricing strategy, and attracting this type of customer. You need to work on your rewards programme, you need to develop it, improve it, and keep an eye on what competitors are doing with their rewards programme.

Focus on the product, on improving the experience that customers have, working on finding ways to become better, and focus on finding the right people – then you will achieve brand loyal customers.

If you are a growing business, you will need both customer loyalty and brand loyalty. You might use some strategies to attract initially the customer with a specific offer, but then convert them into a brand loyal customer because of the product, because of your brand story, because you are investing time and energy to make a change in society in the world. It's not about what is best – customer loyalty or brand loyalty – it's about having both strategies in place, and being conscious and aware that brand loyal clients will help the company grow, spread your brand story, and increase your profitability.

Chapter 10

Winning Hearts

When a boy meets a girl, what happens? Well, there are different boys out there with different agendas. Paul is trying to convince the girl to sleep with him by using 'data' about how great he is and how wealthy he is. James, on the other hand, tells genuine stories about himself and has meaningful conversations about the future and what inspires him. The difference between these boys is that one wants the girl for a one-night stand and the other boy wants to start something meaningful. Most brands behave like horny boys that want to use their customers for a one-night stand many times without investing in building a relationship.

If we ask companies what their customers want, most will say they want quality, price, convenience, features – and they even have the data to prove it. A lot of this has to do with how our brains work: when we communicate, we use logic, and we justify our decisions by using logic, but when we purchase something we use emotions.

We know that the left side of the brain is associated with logical and analytical decisions, and the right side of the brain is associated with creativity and intuition. The emotion part of the brain comes from the limbic system, a group of interconnected structures located deep within the brain.

If we look even further at the brain we can find, on the left side near our ears, the temporal lobe. The limbic system is the whole brain, and the temporal lobe is part of the brain. From that part – the temporal lobe – speech, memory, hearing, vision, behaviour, and emotions fire. Do you see how behaviour and emotions are located in our brain in the same area? It's not a coincidence.

Companies have mastered how to win the mind. They do it by showing us prices, features and benefits. This is how they win the mind. It's easy. It's like giving a treat to Chanel, my dog – all I need to do is pretend I'm opening a bag of treats and she is there. Winning the heart, on the other hand, is hard work. It takes more time, more patience, and it is both an art and science. Storytelling is art. It's art because it's not something that you just pick up one day and immediately master: storytelling requires a blend of skills, not just copywriting, or design, or videography, or some sort of mathematical equation. It's an art because it requires creativity, it requires us to open our minds to possibilities.

We don't like doing the hard work, taking the time needed, because we've been encouraged to believe that we can have everything, today, right now. Want a date for tonight? Swipe right and you might land yourself a date. Feeling hungry? You can have anything you want delivered to you within an hour. Do you want love? Well, that is not for sale and there is no delivery service that can deliver love. You have to work for that.

Look at Amazon. They've mastered how to win the mind – by offering the cheapest, the most convenient way to buy something. You want a book? You can have it the next day, and if that is not fast enough you can have it within seconds on your Kindle. If you are looking for dog poo bags, with a click you can have it, and in the same day. With this offering, Amazon took the crown for being the 'most relevant' company in the UK in 2019: Superbrands, a company that publishes surveys related to brands, reported that Amazon is the business that the British people considered 'most relevant'.

Every year, Superbrands asks 2,500 British shoppers and industry experts to judge 1,500 brands on quality, reliability and distinction. How about 'favourite' brands? For the second year in a row Lego was Britain's favourite brand in 2019. In second place was Apple, followed by Gillette, Rolex, British Airways, Coca-Cola, Andrex, Mastercard, Visa, and

Dyson. I'm not a huge fan of this data and research, for various reasons, but it helps us understand where the mass market is going.

Some brands have won the hearts of their consumers for different reasons, but the point I want to make is that we never see people bragging about how much they love Amazon, and we don't see the Amazon logo on people's arms, do we? We can't even imagine somebody walking with an Amazon logo on their arm, right? What does it mean? What do they stand for? What do they believe in? Do they believe in fast delivery? We don't know. Yet we can see a lot of people with the Apple logo as tattoos or stickers on their cars, laptop cases, and in some cases on their current PC. What about Harley Davidson? In 2019, Harley Davidson sold over 218,000 motorcycles around the world (Statista.com). They have fans, raving fans who are willing to wait from 12 to 24 months to get their custom motorbike.

What about Under Armour? Toms Shoes? Happy Socks? These companies won people's hearts; they have super fans, I would say. But there are plenty of other small companies that have won people's hearts as well.

Huel is another example; they have won people's hearts. Their customers are called 'Hueligans', both by the brand and the customers themselves. In the summer of 2020, Huel held a new product launch in Central London: there was a massive queue to get into the event space, which milled with 'Hueligans'. It's relatively a small company (turnover of £39.8m in 2018/19), yet they've won some people's hearts. I've been a customer for more than two years now, and I never consider looking for an alternative. Even when they increased their product price I didn't think of leaving or look for another brand.

Under Armour is relatively a new company but they took the number 2 slot from Adidas in the US sportswear market by being themselves (Wall Street Journal, 19 December 2019).

The problem I see with a lot of businesses is they look at Nike, Adidas, Dove and others and then try to emulate them. Here's a fact: nobody can be Nike except them. They have their own tone of voice, a way in which they communicate their story. When we try to copy or mimic them, we lose trust with people who are watching. Have you ever met a person who tried to be somebody else? We all have. How do they look? Fake. That's how brands look when they try to mimic somebody else. If we want to win people's hearts, we need to be ourselves. I know it's clichéd advice, but we truly need to be ourselves, otherwise we are depriving ourselves from being loved by people that want to love us.

To win the heart we need to focus on what people are *not* telling us. We need to learn to see what others cannot see. I hear a lot of business people say 'But that's what people tell us they want'. Yes, people tell us what they want, but it doesn't mean that that's why they are buying things. If Henry Ford asked people what they wanted, they would have said they wanted faster horses.

People don't make logical decisions. There are hundreds of examples of this. If people wanted a motorcycle, they would just buy a simple, cheaper one, and not have the Harley-Davidson. If people wanted a good computer, they could have bought one from one of the many computer companies that ultimately went out of business. If people wanted to work from home or outside the office, in isolation, we wouldn't have co-working spaces. If people wanted coffee, they would make coffee at home and not visit coffee shops. A Toyota and a Ferrari will both get you from Central London to Heathrow Airport: the way you will get to the destination is exactly the same way. The things you will see during your trip are exactly the same. The difference is what the person believes about the two brands. The person who drives a Ferrari might say he loves the sound of the engine, or the Italian heritage, or any number of reasons why he owns that car.

People buy feelings, not products. Let me repeat that because it's hard to really comprehend. People buy feelings not products. We think that we are logical human beings making rational decisions. That's what we like to believe and that's what we say. The most basic human needs is the feeling of significance. Brands play a vital role in this area. We might buy something to feel significant and people that say that they don't need anything to feel significant are after the same thing – significance. They are saying that they are so special they don't actually need to buy anything to feel significant.

Harvard Business School professor Gerald Zaltman says that 95 percent of our purchase decision making takes place in the subconscious mind. The subconscious mind plays all kind of tricks with us. We don't even realize it, hence we call it the subconscious mind.

Brands and products are symbols of our beliefs, what we stand for. We associate ourselves with those logos because we want people to believe something about us. Do you think you can convince the most loyal Apple customer to switch to Microsoft or Dell by showing them that the other computer is so much faster, or that it is 10 times the speed, that they will get cash-back, even get a car sticker for them to use? Of course not. That's why Apple don't just have a loyal following, they have a cult. Did you ever notice on the train when somebody opens their Apple computer? They open it with pride, they make sure it's clean and nice. Did you notice a Microsoft or a Dell user open and use their computer the same way an Apple user would? No, no way. Pay attention next time you are in public and see how Apple users use their Macs compared to a Microsoft person. It's two different worlds.

Let's have a look at SoulCycle. The brand has seen exponential growth due to their community-focused mentality, and a small team building a 'media business' (the 'media business' part we will discuss later). The fundamentals are these: when you visit their website you see a tagline, 'Move Your Body, Find Your Soul', and the story, some of which is as follows:

At SoulCycle we aspire to inspire. We inhale intention and exhale expectation. We commit to our climbs and find freedom in our sprints. We are a fitness community raising the roof at our own cardio party. The rhythm pushes us harder than we ever thought possible. Our own strength surprises us every time. Addicted, obsessed, unnaturally attached to our bikes. High on sweat and the hum of the wheel. Core engaged, we reshape our entire bodies, one ride at a time. Change your body take your journey find your soul.

People going to their studios are not just clients; they are fans. There are hundreds of other options to choose from, you can get an indoor bike at home but yet a lot of people prefer their classes because of what they stand for. Surely, if we ask their customers why they go, they are likely to respond with logic, saying it's the instructors, it's the environment, it's anything else that they like. But that's logic. On an emotional level they are more connected with the brand because of their beliefs – the brand's beliefs align with theirs.

The Lululemon brand is striving to be more than just a workout shop. In their words, they "wanted to create a community hub where people could learn and discuss the physical aspects of healthy living, mindfulness and living a life of possibility". It's a great way to look at it.

Yesterday, I went to Nike Town Store on Oxford Street because I wanted a new breathable running top. I thought I would spend no more than £50. While I was in the store, I saw other things than I needed and I ended up spending £150 on Nike products. And I'm a minimalist! How did this happen?

By the way, being a minimalist does not mean I don't buy things, it means that I buy things to use them as 'tools'. I see things as 'tools' to achieve different things I want – I don't buy things just for pleasure or go shopping because I would like a new pair of shoes. This applies everywhere. At my flat, for example, I have three mugs; one mug that I use daily for my coffee and tea, an espresso cup, and a 'guest' mug that I bought from Canada when I visited my father. (Only one 'guest' mug? You might think that I don't invite my friends over, well you are right, I don't, except if I want to sleep with that friend). If you want to learn more about minimalism, I recommend *The Minimalists: Less Is Now* and *Minimalism: A Documentary*, created by The Minimalists, Joshua Fields Milburn and Ryan Nicodemus, and directed by Matt D'Avella.

So, going back to Nike store. Nike, as a brand, convinced me to buy more things because of their product quality and their store structure. The point is, if I was logical, I might have gone to Primark across the street and bought similar things for much less, maybe pay £30 for everything. But I didn't. Because quality matters to me when I run.

We win the heart of a person not by telling them that we want to win their heart, but by showing it. We have so many opportunities to win the heart: with content, showing the customer how we are improving, communicating our story, with amazing customer support, by being empathetic, demonstrating our values.

How do you show that you truly care about the customer? There are many ways, the first step is obviously to have a story and make sure they read and consume the story. Then make sure all your designs and marketing collateral are brilliantly created. Make sure the customer service is a top priority in your company. You may want to create a 'surprise and delight' programme – every month you could choose 10 of your best clients and send them a gift. That gift is not necessarily from your store but something relevant to them.

I recommend you use a good CRM (Customer Relationship Management) tool, so you can keep track of everything and have data on your customers. You might want to send all your great customers a simple 'thank you' card, telling them how much you appreciate them. You might want to create an event and host a special event every month with a guest speaker, you could create monthly Zoom calls. There are almost unlimited ways that we can show that we care. You can create a dedicated blog where you talk about solutions, inspiration and other things that your customers will find valuable.

Winning the heart requires time, dedication and passion, and without these three components we won't be able to do much. We need to care enough to show our customers that we truly care about what we do and that we care enough that we want to find a solution for them. Winning the heart has many benefits when building a meaningful brand. We might not see the results today, but we will definitely see results in the future. It's like going to the gym: we won't be fit from day one, we need to be consistent.

If we want to win the heart we have to behave like a gentleman, ask the girl out, be kind and loving, tell the truth even when we mess up, be authentic, go above and beyond and propose to the girl. By being a man that truly cares about the girl, we win their heart.

CHAPTER **11**

Telling Your Brand Story

Like storytelling, 'content marketing' is a term that is overused and misunderstood. When you say you do 'content marketing' people assume that you make TikTok videos or write blog articles. Both of these assumptions could be right. But we can say that a documentary on Netflix is content, a book is content, a Facebook post is content. A lot of things could be called 'content'.

Lexico.com (produced by Oxford University Press) describes content marketing as:

> ... *a type of marketing that involves the creation and sharing of online material (such as videos, blogs, and social media posts) that does not explicitly promote a brand but is intended to stimulate interest in its products or services.*

Wikipedia tells us that content marketing is *'a form of marketing focused on creating, publishing, and distributing content for a targeted audience online'.*

The US-based Content Marketing Institute, founded in 2007, says:

> *Content marketing is a strategic marketing approach focused on creating and distributing valuable, relevant, and consistent content to attract and retain a clearly defined audience — and, ultimately, to drive profitable customer action.*

You can see how each definition is different.

What does great, valuable content mean to me? *Creating content that adds value to a specific group of people in four ways: to inspire, educate, entertain or help them make a better purchasing decision. The goal of great content should be always helping the desired audience. It should help people connect and understand the brand more and it should make the desired audience (potential customers) feel better or enlightened.*

In today's world, it's astonishing how many opportunities we have to create and distribute content. We can start a blog or a YouTube channel, launch a podcast, broadcast on TikTok, use Instagram, and many other things.

The way meaningful businesses grow today is nowhere close to how iconic brands were built.

When I started working with fashion influencer Sade (@s4de_u) in 2016, she had just started her Instagram, with fewer than 10 followers. Today she has over 105,000 real followers on her personal account and 144,000 on her brand account, The Kemist. For a year, she created high quality content that added value to her audience. I have to say she is very talented in what she does, extraordinary, even, and you can see that in her content. She created a small fashion brand, and those that follow her love her, they've become fans of hers and the brand. This didn't happen by accident, it happened because she planned, she worked, still does work very hard, and with a content-first approach.

There is a huge difference between creating product-based content and value-based content. Product-based content, I sometimes call it ego-driven content because it's all about the brand. The reason it's ego-driven is because that type of content doesn't add any value to the consumer – it's great if somebody is ready to buy that product, but not everybody is ready to buy.

Every single booking, every single purchase, has a buying cycle. A buying cycle is a process that each one of us goes through when making a purchasing decision. The most basic buying cycle is the following: Awareness, Consideration, Interest, Preference and Purchase. We all go through the cycle every single time we buy something. When items are less valuable, a toothbrush, for instance, the time we spend in the buying cycle is much shorter. On the other hand, if it is a hotel room, we spend much more time in the buying cycle until we make the decision.

For example, I'm in the market for a running watch, and have been for the past two months. I'm in the Preference stage, because I don't know which brand to choose and what model to choose. I posted a question on a private ultra-running Facebook group about which watch should I get – Garmin or Suunto, including two models from each brand, with a price range from £340 to £730. I got 47 people respond within an hour with their recommendations. Now, my problem is that the features are similar, or even the same, and I find Garmin's story is a bit fuzzy. I understand that they were in the GPS business and then expanded into watches, but that doesn't say what they believe in. Their story doesn't differentiate them. I don't mind buying from Suunto if they can give me something that I can relate to. Two huge corporations are losing out opportunities. I could have bought the watch already, but the number of options (from both sides) are just overwhelming, and now I'm not really bothered anymore. So we as consumers are in different places in different times. We can't treat every single person, every follower on social media, as if they are ready to buy tomorrow.

Ego-driven content is liked by the marketing team and by the owner, but it's not adding any value to the follower. It's important to create content that will make the consumer think and feel something. It might be that you are educating the consumer about something, it might be that you are entertaining. Testimonials help brands establish trust, but can appear alongside other types of content. This is where the content strategy comes in.

'Just add more value' has become a cliché. Some people might think that value is speaking about their services, some might think testimonials are valuable. Some hoteliers think that posting on Instagram about their hotel views is valuable. I don't know about you, I love seeing spectacular views, but when every single post on Instagram is a view? It is boring, to say the least.

Posting articles and inspirational quotes all day will not drive business results. To create great content, we need a content strategy that is focused on the customer and on the business.

The solution is to look at your story, look at the problems the company solves, and keep these things in mind when building a content strategy. You might say for the next 30 days you will create 10 blog articles that will explain to customers and potential customers how they can improve their healthy habits, and 10 creative artworks for social media to promote those articles so people visit the website and read them. Then perhaps you can create a GIF to promote the article with targeted Facebook and Instagram ads.

There is a way to frame a story – when you have your main brand story, you create other stories around it to use for your content. For example, there is the founder's story, there is the 'How I joined the brand' story: there are so many events you can choose from and share them with content. But we can't just start bragging and sharing our stories in every single post – it will look premeditated and unnatural. We can be strategic about it. Content gives us the opportunity to create seeds, to connect with the other person on a human level.

The execution is really important. By execution, I mean the tone of voice, designs, and what type of content we post. You can make a podcast, for example, and then take 60 seconds from your podcast, edit a part that was intriguing, and post that bit on social – this is micro-content, to promote your podcast on social media. You can go further by promoting that micro-content using targeted social media ads.

There are so many talented people out there, with great advice and valuable insights, yet the execution of their content is appalling. As an example, I was looking for an accountant, one who is different, unique, rather than the usual corporate accountant. I found one, his wording was different – kudos to him – but his web and social designs were horrendous. Unbearable to look at them. I was a potential customer, and I did not want to work with him – if he was 'saving money' using cheap agencies or freelancers to do his work, I can imagine how my accounts will be done. No, thank you. But he is not alone – there are so many talented people out there, yet their aesthetics and designs are horrible. And a story is non-existent.

It's important that we know who we want to target. You might want to create an ebook and promote that ebook to your potential customers. That ebook can have interesting data from your industry, or upcoming trends, or maybe you include opinions about your industry or solutions to a problem we face. An ebook is an opportunity to build credibility and your email list.

The goal is to become a content hub. Yes, if we want to truly succeed in this day and age, we need to think of ourselves as media companies. Create a strategy where you focus on creating valuable content that people want to consume.

Newsletters should be our primary focus. We need to build our list. And I don't mean building some kind of 'funnel'. No, I mean creating a daily, weekly or monthly newsletter where you share your insights, ideas and knowledge with people. Use social media to promote that newsletter. The goal is to create content that people want to receive, want to hear. I'm sure you have certain newsletters or people that you want to hear from. The question we should ask ourselves is 'What will happen if we stopped creating and publishing content? Will people miss us? Will they notice that we are gone?'

A great example of missing somebody is when I stopped receiving Seth Godin's newsletters. Seth Godin is one of the best marketers and authors out there. Every day he sends a newsletter; it is his blog, with a thought, an idea, a concept. At some point, I realised that it had been days since I had received anything. I immediately emailed his team to find out why. I even save his emails in a dedicated folder, so I can go back to them whenever I'm in need of inspiration.

Every Monday, I get a newsletter from Mark Manson, a self-help author and blogger. He named his newsletter Mindf*ck Monday. His promise is that every week he will send you three potential life-changing ideas to help you become a slightly less awful human being. The newsletter's name is exactly what you would expect from Mark Manson – he is the author of *The Subtle Art of Not Giving A F*ck and Everything Is F*cked: A Book About Hope*.

A content strategy should support your newsletter, and amplify your story in different forms of content. Then we can start building an emotional connection with our audience. And by audience I mean humans that might buy something from us, humans that are potential clients. If you think about it, they are already giving something to us, something that has a very high value – their attention and time. We need to respect that and appreciate the fact that people consuming our content are investing their time with us.

The best strategy to help us increase sales and build loyalty is to make that switch from being product focused to being value and content focused. So promoting our content to get people to come to us and, in a way, a good way, get hooked. Not everybody is going to like it, not everybody is going to share it but when they do, they become loyal – and that is gold.

Create an advert for your content, promote your content, and then use all your energy on creating more amazing content. There are so many benefits to building an audience rather than just clients. The first benefit is that once you have built an audience, you are more likely to sell to them a product or service that is relevant to them. The customer acquisition cost (CAC) is going to be so much lower when we have an audience rather than promote our products and services. That's why it's important to know your customer lifetime value (CLV) because then we can make better business and marketing decisions. A lot of companies and hotels go after customers with a very low CLV. They are not really worth it, because they don't value the same things you value, and the amount you spend on acquiring those clients is better spent acquiring customers with higher CLV.

Once we understand the value of our customer, and we start creating content for them, it's so much more effective because you are engaging with them. When they are ready to book a hotel room, or book a reservation at that restaurant, or buy that product or service, who do you think will be the first company they will contact? Yours, of course.

In his famous book *How to Win Friends and Influence People,* Dale Carnegie said that you have to be genuinely interested in other people. I would add that you need to be interesting, as well. When somebody chooses and looks at our content they need to be intrigued, and want more of what they see.

There are companies that charge for content - that's their business model. You can give out samples of your content and then ask people to follow or subscribe for 'premium' content. A great example of this is how I discovered a great podcast. A small segment was available on Apple Podcasts, but if you wanted to listen to full episodes you needed to go and pay a subscription on Luminary. Luminary is a subscription podcast network with original shows; it wants to become the Netflix of the podcasting world. This is an example of how audiences are willing to pay money to consume content in a world full of free podcasts and shows.

Another example is a YouTube video I watched because I wanted to improve my skills in writing creative briefs. I watched two videos by a strategy guy - he is consulting brands like Spotify, Coke, Apple and others - and I knew that I wanted to learn more from him. He has an academy where you join and pay a membership. I saved the link, I took his free course, I liked it, learned from it, implemented the idea, and, a month later, I signed up for the academy. Once I'm done, I will send my designer on the course, as well.

Then there is The Hustle Co, a daily business newsletter which recently launched a new weekly subscriber-only newsletter called Trends (trends.co). For £299 a year, subscribers get access to news and content about start-ups, companies, and business personalities.

There are hundreds of other platforms and premium content that we can see and learn from. The question we need to be asking is 'If we charged for our content, would people pay for it?'

Let's ask another one… 'How we can create so much value that our audience would actually pay for it?'

Chapter 12

Wired to Belong

Yesterday I went for a run to Hyde Park Corner. I wore a yellow t-shirt on top of my running top. The yellow t-shirt is from Dogs Trust, a charity that helps abandoned dogs (they run 21 rehoming centres to save over 16,000 abandoned dogs a year). The t-shirt included their logo and a slogan, 'A dog is for life'. While I ran my 15km, I might have passed hundreds of people. Some of them may have read what was on the t-shirt; others did not notice it. Some of them read it and 'liked' me more without knowing me: they just felt connected to me in some small way because they might have a dog, love dogs, or are animal lovers.

If I'm sitting in a co-working space, and there are two people working opposite me, one working on a Mac and one working on a Dell, immediately I feel more connected to the person using the Mac. The Mac user might by rude, obnoxious, stupid, but without opening their mouth I made a positive assumption about them.

When you travel abroad and you hear somebody speak your language – you might be in Cyprus and you overhear a British person in the supermarket speak – immediately you *like* them more. When I'm on the Underground and I hear people speak in Cypriot Greek, I instantly feel more connected to them than the other fifty people on that train.

If I tell somebody that I'm vegan, immediately the other person is going to like me or hate me. It depends on what views the other person holds. If I tell somebody that I support mental health for men, and the other person is passionate about it, or lost a loved one because of mental health, they may like me more.

These assumptions are made on a subconscious level. They are not something that we think consciously off.

Why is that? Why do we have these feelings? Well, it's simple. We as humans are wired to belong. It's in our survival mechanism. It's a very basic human need. The need to belong is not logical, it's emotional. This need does not exist only in the United Kingdom or Europe - it's everywhere, in all cultures. It's basically a feeling we get when we see the other person share our values and beliefs. The reason we want to be connected is because it makes us feel safe. And we all want to feel safe.

We trust those with whom we are able to perceive common values and beliefs. And this desire is what drives us to do a lot of irrational things. We spend money to get that feeling, but our conscious brain will not tell us that we are spending money to get that feeling, and we will not tell others that, 'You know, I am buying this particular brand of shoes because I want to feel safe and belong.' Of course not, it doesn't work that way.

How do you think fan clubs start out? What about football club supporters? They share the same beliefs. There are families that support different football clubs and they hate each other - why? Because of 11 players running around a pitch for a ball. Players that get paid millions. If somebody gives a player one or two more millions, they will leave that football club. It all sounds like business to me.

There is a saying that Seth Godin uses a lot in his work: 'People like us, do things like this'. More than getting features or benefits, we are driven to become a member of good standing in the tribe. We want to be respected by those we aspire to connect with, we want to know what we ought to do, we want to be part of that circle. Not the norms of the masses, but the norms of our chosen tribe.

There is an internal narrative accompanying all that we say and do. We might wear a white t-shirt, a blazer, or a nice pair of shoes because we tell ourselves we look good and we are comfortable, but it is also because it's what a successful version of ourselves would wear.

Belonging is a feeling; it's not something that we can explain. It's something that is very deep inside of us, something we can't put into words. For example, if Dell started selling cars how would that feel? Weird, right? We would be surprised. How about Apple? If Apple started selling cars, how would that feel? An iCar? It would feel okay. The reason why is because Dell defines itself as a computer company, Apple defines itself as a company that has a purpose, a mission, and many products can sit within that mission.

I'm sure a lot of people would buy cars from Apple. Actually, it is pretty much an open secret that Apple is working on a car (Reuters.com December 21, 2020). We don't know exactly if it will be a self-driving car or an electric car, but we know that by 2024 we might see iCars on the road.

When Julian Hearn started Huel in June 2015, his mission statement was simple: "To make nutritionally complete, convenient, affordable food, with minimal impact on animals and the environment."

People, including myself, believe in what the company stands for. When I see another person wearing the black Huel t-shirt or hoodie I immediately feel more connected to them because they support the same vision. We have a common belief. Actually, a couple of months ago, someone started a conversation randomly with me, on the street, about Huel. It was because, I believe, wearing a black Huel t-shirt. We had a brief chat and we felt connected, in a way.

When we feel that we belong, we feel we are part of a mission that is bigger than us. We want to feel that our tribe, or our people, are on to something. The reason why a lot of people write in their Instagram bio about the different things that they do and like is because they identify with those things – their identity depends on them.

If we look at our human needs, we will find that 'belonging' is in the top five. According to the twentieth century humanist psychologist Abraham Maslow, all our actions are motivated in order to achieve certain needs we have. Maslow first introduced the concept of hierarchy of needs in his 1943 paper 'A Theory of Human Motivation', and his subsequent book *Motivation and Personality*. His work shows us that humans are motivated to fulfil basic needs before moving on the other needs, more advanced needs, you might say.

Abraham Maslow's hierarchy is most often displayed as a pyramid. At its base are the most basic needs, and the most complex needs are at the top.

The most basic needs are physiological – the need for food, water, sleep and warmth. Once these are met, humans move on to the next needs: safety and security. Once we feel safe and secure, we look to fulfil a need for belonging, which comes in different forms – love, family, friends, community groups, religious organisations, and intimacy. This is why some people become depressed and have anxiety problems: they don't feel loved and accepted by other people. Relationships with friends and family matter a lot, and partners play a huge role. This is where people get involved in activism, sports teams, religious groups, and group activities.

As we progress up the pyramid, we look for appreciation and respect. This is the fourth need and is called *Esteem*. At this point it's very important for humans to gain respect and appreciation from others. That's why we want to be recognised for the efforts we put. People want to feel that they are valued and are making a contribution in this world. That's why we participate in competitions, and have hobbies (photography, weightlifting, swimming, and so on).

The last, and most advanced, need is self-actualization. This is a need that humans have to achieve their full potential as human beings. Maslow defined self-actualization as follows:

It may be loosely described as the full use and exploitation of talents, capabilities, potentialities, etc. Such people seem to be fulfilling themselves and to be doing the best that they are capable of doing. They are people who have developed or are developing to the full stature of which they are capable.

Self-actualizing people are very self-aware, they want to grow, and they are interested in fulfilling their potential.

His theory was very popular in the psychology world, but received a lot of criticism as well. There are individuals that say that there is not enough research to support his theory. In 2011, a study published by University of Illinois tried to put the hierarchy to the test. They found that fulfilment of the needs was strongly correlated with happiness. Further, they found that people from different cultures all over the world reported that self-actualization and social needs were important even when many of the most basic needs were unfulfilled.

There are other studies and experts who have studied our needs. American author, coach and philanthropist Tony Robbins defined six human needs. After studying what motivates humans for 40 years, he says that every single human must feel the following to survive:

1. Certainty: assurance you can avoid pain and gain pleasure
2. Uncertainty/variety: the need for the unknown, change, new stimuli
3. Significance: feeling unique, important, special or needed
4. Connection/love: a strong feeling of closeness or union with someone or something
5. Growth: an expansion of capacity, capability or understanding
6. Contribution: a sense of service and focus on helping, giving to and supporting others

In Robbins' theory, connection and love is number four: it acknowledges that we as human beings want to be connected. That's why we see people being fans of football clubs, and brands. We identify with them.

What causes humans to take action and make a decision to buy? Aristotle answered this question many years ago in his treatise *Rhetoric,* which dates back to the fourth century BCE. This is one of his most famous quotes:

> "All human actions have one or more of these seven causes: chance, nature, compulsion, habit, reason, passion and desire."

Each 'cause' he identified has a direct correlation to our buying decisions.

Change

We might stumble across something without any purpose behind it. We might have liked something on a website and decided to buy it. For example, in my bathroom I have a book, *Things To Do While You Poo* by Hugh Jassburn.

Nature

Sometimes we buy things because we are forced to by nature. For example, if I'm walking down the street and it starts raining, I may rush into a supermarket and buy an umbrella.

Compulsion

This is a huge one - a lot of purchasing decisions happen because of this. We buy based on desire and instinct. The irrational behaviour moved us through the buying cycle very fast.

Habit

We all know this one. We go to a nearby grocery store because it is our habit. We are likely to keep shopping at certain stores because we are humans and humans are habitual by nature. We shop there for comfort and consistency.

Reasoning

Some purchasing decisions are made because we thought it through, did our research, identified what we needed exactly, and made the purchase. I wanted to track my weight, I looked it up on the web, found suitable 'smart' weighing scales, read some reviews and bought it. Simple.

Passion

This one is when our emotions influence us to buy, when we are triggered by an emotional experience. These purchases satisfy our feelings in some way.

Desire

When we simply have the desire for that pair of shoes – we just want it like the kid in the checkout queue wanting a chocolate bar. Without logic or rational thinking, we can have that intense feeling of wanting and desiring.

If humans want to belong, why not create a space for people to join? This is an opportunity for brands to create a story, a narrative that people will be able to follow and believe.

This is how movements start: they have a common goal, a common belief, and they march through it.

In 2020 we saw protests heralded by Black Lives Matter, all over the world. In Manchester, 15,000 people joined one protest, walking and expressing their opinion about racism. They believe in something: they want to end racism. They want a better world.

Every year in the spring, more than 10,000 people join the Official Animal Rights March organised by Surge. The purpose of the march is to unite the vegan community globally and inspire vegans to become active. The march began in London in 2016 and it is now hosted in Canada, France, USA and other major cities. Some people carry banners, showing what we as humans do to animals for a meal. What all those people have in common is that they belong to a community and they want to make change happen. They *are* making change happen - the number of vegans in the UK quadrupled between 2014 and 2019 to more than 600,000, or 1.16% of the population. Another huge affront to carnivorous conventions is Veganuary – a challenge to eat only plant-based foods for a month. In 2017, Veganuary had less than 100,000 people signing up, and in January 2021 there were more than 500,000 people. We can see a huge change in our world, because of activism, social media, documentaries, and people opening their minds.

Chapter 13

Don't be Boring

I was in the Picasso Museum in Barcelona, walking around, looking at the paintings, reading the titles and the stories behind the paintings, when I saw, on my left, a woman take her two hands, make them one whole, and look at a painting through them – with one eye, like a binocular. I don't know why she did that, but I found it interesting how we might have the same painting in front of us, but see it in different ways.

You might say its taste, or opinion. Which is very true. Yet if we look at something objectively, we can all agree when we see something was done with passion - we can see when something is created with care. Personally, I'm not familiar with art, and I'm ignorant in that sense – I have no idea what each painting is – but as ignorant as I am in that department, when I looked at Picasso's work I felt inspired. I saw the passion and the creativity in his work.

On Oxford Street in London we have more than a hundred shops within two and half kilometres. There are some fantastic, global brands with shops there, but during the holiday season there is one shop that always has people taking pictures by its windows: Selfridges. You knew that, I know you knew that! When I ran past Selfridges, en route to Hyde Park, there were around fifty people out there taking pictures of their shop front. Out of all those shops, Selfridges is winning the game in the most competitive street in London, or even in the UK, if I might say it.

On a daily basis we live on autopilot; our brain's job is to make sure we survive and we don't waste all of our energy. The brain wants to make things 'automatic' as soon as possible. Even when ordering our coffee, we go to our favourite coffee shop, we greed the barista, we say 'Good morning', we order our latte with almond milk, we wait and we leave when our latte is ready. A whole process 'saved' in our system.

Can you imagine if we had to think about how to get to work every morning? We wouldn't last a day in this world. We have a place where we put things at home, at our office. That's why we put our keys at home in a specific place, so we don't think about it all the time. When our keys are not in their usual place, we panic. Did we put them somewhere else? What happened?

Yet when we travel to a new location we check the map 10 times, we check our phones, we observe everything, we are more aware of our surroundings. We are more present when we are in a new city because our brain is not on autopilot: our brain is looking at things for the first time.

In order to capture somebody's attention we need to break their pattern. The keyword is *pattern*. We can debate whether mass market taste over the years has changed, and we can see patterns that indicate our taste in some areas has declined, but we can agree that when we see something that is creative, and something that has taken time to create, we appreciate it.

When we see something different, we notice it. Creativity gives us an unfair advantage. We all have creativity and we all can use creativity. Airbnb started a movement towards out-of-the-ordinary accommodation, with people looking for boutique hotels, independent creative hotels and homely apartments. Companies like Brew Dog and Camden Town Brewery have grown exponentially in the past ten years. We have websites like Etsy and Folksy that act as marketplaces for individual artists, and DeviantArt, a thriving online art community.

Several years ago, at Harvard University, Christopher Chabris and Daniel Simons ran an experiment known as the 'Invisible Gorilla' experiment. The experiment included six people dressed in white shirts and three people dressed in black shirts passing basketballs around. While people watched the video, they had to count the number of passes made by the people in white shirts. At some point a gorilla comes into the middle of the action, looks at the camera and thumps its chest, and then casually leaves. The gorilla spends nine seconds on screen. When people were asked beforehand if they would see the gorilla, almost everyone answered 'Yes, of course I would.' How can you miss the gorilla? Come on, me? I would see the freaking gorilla in the middle of the screen. They found that half of the people watching the video and counting the passes missed the gorilla in the middle of the screen. It was like the gorilla was invisible. We can learn one thing from this experiment: we are not aware of a lot of things that are around us and we don't even know that we are missing so much. This is called inattentional blindness. When we are doing a task, working, walking towards the Tube, our brain is focused on achieving one task. When we break the pattern, we must make sure that it's worth it for the consumer to give us his attention, otherwise it is just breaking the pattern and annoying the consumer.

The problem that a lot of company's face is that most of them are the same: they are not differentiating themselves. We don't need to go far – let's just step out and see what's happening on the street. Most stores are boring. They are beyond boring. And I mean everybody: off licenses, grocery stores, restaurants, gyms, coffee shops, retail stores, hotels, dry cleaners. And I don't just mean small companies, I include the big guys, as well. What is different about them? Most are the same. That's why we don't pay attention. That's why the cost of acquiring a customer (CAC) is going up every year. Our attention span goes down, we don't pay attention, our time is limited, responsibilities and other aspects of our modern world come into play and we become masters at avoiding advertising, we become masters at avoiding things that don't matter to us.

I hate boring, I really do. I get really frustrated when I see people that have so many interesting things to say and do, yet they communicate and they send 'boring' signals. Even in dating, I'm bored to death seeing women who are apparently doing a copy and paste of each other's biographies on dating apps. One says 'I like pizza' – really? You like pizza? Or the ever popular 'I'm looking for a travel buddy.' If we look at a hundred profiles on any dating app we will see that most are very similar.

Life is really short, and we shouldn't waste it by not trying new things, by not pushing our creative boundaries. Don't get me wrong, I do a lot of boring things myself – you might find running boring. That's fine, it's okay, we don't need to find everything that others do exciting – we just need to find things that excite us and communicate our excitement about the things we do. So if you ask me about things that I do, I'm not going to communicate to you and say 'yeah, running is cool' in the most monotonous tones. No, I will say 'I freaking love running, you can connect with nature, explore new streets, explore new cities, breathe fresh air, discover more about yourself, do gratitude runs, do sprint runs, connect with people, sign up for challenges, listen to music, push yourself and so much more', and say it with passion, with conviction. Some people say skydiving is boring. I have to disagree, and recommend they try it at least once. Skydiving is one of the best things that a human being can experience.

How do we stand out, then? Well, our story should be the foundation of how we stand out. But once we have our story and our slogan, we need to execute it in a creative way. You can say 'Create a better tomorrow' casually, or you can say 'Create a better tomorrow' with conviction, and explain that we all can have a better tomorrow if we do the work in a better way. You can use creativity in your business, and not just in your marketing and communication – I mean everywhere. In your product, in your customer service.

In December, a lot of companies send Christmas gifts to their customers and suppliers. Outside of corporate, most of us are buying Christmas presents during this period. To put that in numbers, for those of you who are detailed and number orientated: in the UK, consumers spent £78.6 billion pounds in six weeks from November to December 2018, an increase of 2.17% from 2017*.

What if we sent a gift to a friend, loved one or customer in March? How much impact will it have? You could write a card saying that you saw this gift and decided to buy it for him or her because you were thinking about them. Do you think they will pause and ask 'Why did he send me a gift?' Yes, they will. Do you think it will make a bigger impact? Yes, it will.

I have a rule with my friends, family, and my romantic relationships. Because I'm a minimalist, I don't believe that a gift will show that I care about them or that I love them – it's just a gift, anybody could buy it. My gift to them is me being present with them: when we speak, when we meet, I'm there 100%. I don't send birthday gifts; I don't send Christmas gifts. I *might* do, sometimes, but it is rare. Not because I'm stingy, but because I think that love and our time is the most important gift.

This doesn't mean that I don't buy gifts at all. If I see something that a friend of mine needs, I will buy it. For example, I have a friend that loves coffee. I believe that if you like coffee and want quality coffee, you need to get an espresso machine, so I bought him Nespresso machine as a gift. It wasn't his birthday, it wasn't New

Year, it was a regular day in May. For my mum, for example, I didn't buy her a gift in years, but this year I bought her a ticket for one of Tony Robbins' events (UPW), which is potentially life changing. Another friend had a problem with his phone. I asked him why he never used an iPhone. He said he wouldn't pay £1,000 to buy an iPhone. I bought him a new iPhone as a gift; it was close to his birthday. I will not be giving him a gift for the next five years! I've got that covered. I'm joking, of course, but the point is that when we do things unexpectedly, people appreciate it more.

Companies are obsessed with data, and use and abuse emails to send more and more sales campaigns and spam the hell the out of them. The objective is obviously to increase sales, to increase referrals and so on. But how about sending a simple, 'thank you' card with a small *unbranded* gift? I'm a customer like yourself at many brands yet I haven't received one single card from any of them. I have received vouchers and the 'We missed you' card. When I get those cards and emails, they make me laugh because instead of 'We missed you', they could have written 'We missed your cash'.

Being different requires us to take action, and it requires some thought. If we don't really care about the industry, the problem we are solving, then all this will look like a lot of hard work. We can say that we are different or we can show that we are different, the former doesn't really work.

Whatever we do, we must avoid at all costs being boring because being boring will cost us much more than being different. We notice things that are outlandish. When things are different we speak about them, we share them, we tell our friends about them – that is 'word of mouth', or, you might say, 'free advertising from a trusted source'.

CHAPTER **14**

How a Story Can Increase Your Sales

Do stories really have an impact on the bottom line? Is it really worth it, putting this much energy and financial investment into this slightly intangible thing, 'storytelling'? I speak a lot about making an impact, and doing the right thing but we all have invoices to pay, salaries to pay, bills to pay, and we need make money, right? I agree with you, 100%. You might not believe it, but I love making money. Making money is a great way of keeping score, they say.

The way I think about money is that it is a tool, a tool we can use to either make things good, or make things worse. It is a tool, an energy. The problem is when we become obsessed with just making money, we get blindfolded and don't see the bigger picture.

A few years ago, I had a moment where I was broke, completely broke - mentally, physically and financially. One night I went to sleep with zero in my bank account and when I woke up I received a payment of £10,000 from a client. I didn't really feel any better – I was the same person as I was yesterday. It made me think about what I had heard at an event I attended just a few months earlier. The speaker said something that stuck with me, he said, 'We value ourselves based on how much we have in our bank account'. It took a lot of time for me to truly understand that I'm not defined by my bank account. Today, I get it.

I learnt a lot from a book I read called; *Money: Know More, Make More, Give More* by Rob Moore. I understood that money is not evil, it's not bad, it's actually a very good thing. If we can make more money, we can use it to improve a lot of things – starting with ourselves. That's why I want to make more money, to increase my sales, and why I want to become financially educated. The way we do that is by adding value to this world. Money is an exchange, it's an exchange of perceived value.

If we can add more value to the universe, we will be rewarded, but the key is not to think or come from a perspective that is obsessed with getting paid. We should be obsessed with adding value, and make 'more money' is a by-product of this. I believe it's about being intentional and genuinely wanting to add more value to other people. In our case we are talking about business, so it means we need to add more value to our customers by improving the product, by being ethical and by putting creativity into what we do.

Perceived value is different for everyone. Some people find convenience and saving time valuable. Yesterday, I was waiting for the train at Kings Cross station when a lady came up to me and asked how she can get to Paddington. The Piccadilly line was suspended, so from there (Paddington) she planned to get an overground train to Heathrow airport. I told her that it's easier to use the Heathrow Express service from Paddington, and she said 'That's expensive'. Cost was her reason for using an overground train. I said 'Well, an average ticket will cost you £20 but you will be there much quicker and there is less risk in missing your flight.' Isn't £20 cheaper than a new plane ticket to Canada?

Perceived value is abstract, and open to interpretation, but how companies use it is astounding, and highly effective. Perceived value is the worth a product or service has in a consumer's mind. The customer's perceived value of a product or service determines how much he or she is willing to pay for it. Customer-perceived value is also called *value in marketing.* Perceived value is subjective, based on qualitative measures such as emotional, social and cultural factors.

Let's imagine a pair of white shoes in a plain shopping bag without any logos. What are those shoes like? Now let's imagine now the exact same pair of shoes in a Harrods bag. You can use them for the same activities as the other pair of shoes, but in our mind we think that the shoes in the Harrods bag are superior, higher quality. With the pair of shoes from Harrods, we have new perceptions, our expectations are different, our feelings towards those pair of shoes are more positive and we would be able to pay extra. Of course, we don't know what brand is in Harrods bag, because Harrods is not a shoe company. Let's say in that bag we had a pair of Balenciaga shoes. One pair of shoes might cost £575. Do I think the quality of their shoes are better than my £100 Nike shoes? No. I've never bought them, and I don't know much about the brand. In my eyes, the perceived value is different from somebody who bought them and is wearing them.

There are hundreds of examples like that. We perceive things differently, if we want quality, we will happily pay more. Features alone will not do the job, that's why packaging is important if we want to increase the brands perceived value.

When I receive something from Moo, a commercial printer in London, I smile because they always add an interesting sticker, and their packaging is always spot on. Well-designed packaging and convenience is more appealing than a low price

There is another factor that we need to consider – prestige. This is a huge factor. Customers want the feeling of prestige. Why do you think we have so many people buy fake luxury goods? Look at Instagram – it's filled with fake Chanel and Louis Vuitton products. Actually, the counterfeit industry nets £1.2 trillion globally every year. Some people would never buy a fake product, yet others buy them all the time. Balenciaga is a prestigious brand; people that care about prestige buy them.

What is the difference between a Domino's Pizza and a frozen pizza from a supermarket? Do you think there is a difference in quality? I say 'Of course, there is a huge difference in quality.' But that's me. Domino's Pizza is likely to cost around £20, a frozen supermarket pizza might cost a pound. Some people will say that the frozen supermarket pizza is much better. In their minds, they are right. Maybe they think it being only a pound, it's great – compared to what they can do by themselves at home. Purezza Pizza in Camden offers one of the highest quality vegan pizzas, in my opinion. Some people will disagree with that because they never tried it, or they might not know anything about the brand. Taste and perceived value are in play here.

Another great example is the Ted's Grooming Room, a group of luxury barbershops established by Ted Baker. A friend told me that I 'waste' £50 having my hair done there. I ask him why he thought it was a waste, and he replied that he gets his hair for 'a tenner' at a barber down the road. Surely, it's a deal I can't miss, right? In this department, we don't see eye to eye. I perceive Ted's Grooming Room to be much higher quality, a better service, and it just *feels* better. The thing is, the barber down the road might be as qualified as Ted Baker's barber, right? Maybe they even went to the same hair salon academy. But I perceive Ted's Grooming Room to be much better. I have to say I tried once to go to the barber down the road. When I had just moved to Hendon in North London, I needed grooming, but was in a hurry, and I didn't want to get the train and go to Central London. So, I had a haircut in Hendon with a local barber. Was it better? No. Was it worse? Yes. The guy rushed, and I didn't get the treatment I'm used to getting. He didn't wash my hair properly and he didn't do the sides properly. You see I know nothing about hair, but throughout the years I notice how Ted Bakers' barbers do my hair - I'm looking at them all the freaking time, you really can't *not* look at what they do because you have the mirror in front of you! This guy butchered my hair. I paid a tenner.

The author of the book The Brand Gap Marty Neumeier sums up what a brand is quite eloquently, he says that a brand is a person's gut feeling about a product, a service, or a company. It's a gut feeling because we're all emotional, intuitive beings, despite our best efforts to be rational. It's a person's gut feeling, because in the end the brand is defined by individuals, not by companies, markets, or the so-called general public.

That's why it's so important to understand who we want to target. It's one of the first things we need to do: think about our customers. Who do we want to target? Because if we target everyone – people with different taste, people that don't value time, or quality, or craftsmanship, we will lose resources, time, and energy. There are some people that are cheap and lack a sense of taste in some areas because this is how they think and how they grew up. Taste is something that you can learn, it's a skill. Ten years ago, my taste in design was absolutely horrific, it was non-existent. Throughout the years I had an open mind and I learned from people who had better taste. It's okay that some people have bad taste, that's them. It's how they view the world, and it is absolutely fine.

How about stories? What difference do they make? Well, the reason why we buy certain things is because we tell ourselves a story, to justify an emotional part of the brain. As we discussed earlier, we all make emotional decisions. We tell stories to ourselves about a certain product, a certain brand. Even when we say 'I want the cheapest underwear', we tell ourselves a story, 'I'm a kind of a person that doesn't care about…' underwear, food, hotels, coffee, clothes, whatever the category the product is in.

One of my favourite experiments was done by two American journalists Rob Walker and Joshua Glenn back in 2009. They wanted to determine if a story would affect the sale of a product. They bought different products from thrift stores and garage sales. An average product cost them less than a pound, and in total they spend £93.83 ($128.74) to buy all the products. All the products they purchased were ordinary – a toy pink horse, a bottle opener, a wooden mallet, a jar of marbles, and so on.

Then they asked volunteer writers to write short purpose-written stories for each item. Once they had all the stories, they put all items on eBay and instead of displaying a routine description of the product, they included the story that the authors wrote. They made sure it was clear in the description that the story was fictional, so any consumer could see that the object on sale was not more special than the common household item it appeared to be. Within five months, everything was sold. What they paid less than one hundred pounds for was sold on eBay for a total of £2,644.75 ($3,612.51) - an increase of 2,800% in value.

This is what Walker and Glenn said: "Narratives transforms insignificant objects into significant ones." Basically, cheap objects became valuable.

The Brand Storytelling Report 2015 found that nearly eight out of 10 UK adults wanted brands to tell stories as part of their marketing. The report, commissioned by Headstream, a content marketing agency, revealed that while the call for storytelling is strong, 85% of the 2,000 adults surveyed couldn't give an example of a memorable story told by a brand. 38% of those surveyed wanted to see stories about regular people or brand customers, and just 10% want to hear the story of the brand's CEO or the founder.

When people were asked where they preferred to see brand stories online, this was most likely to be website content, blog, or email newsletter. In second place was website advertising, third place social media advertising, in the number four slot was a brand's social media account, number five, shared by a friend, number six was a blog feature on another website, and last of these was a messaging app.

The same research reported that if people liked your brand story, 55% were more likely to buy the product in the future, 44% will share the story and 15% will buy the product immediately. We want more stories, we are yearning for more interesting stories that will inspire us, and educate us, and we are willing to pay more for that.

Many millennials – sometimes called Generation Y - avoid buying from brands that don't stand up for something. They do their research, and they make it very clear – if you don't stand up for something, they are not buying it. They prefer to spend more, in some cases, just to be part of a movement. Some people might say that this is not how everybody behaves and thinks, and that's okay – we don't need everybody, we just need people that are willing to embrace what we are selling.

We are all tired of ads trying to convince us that this new shampoo is the best shampoo for us. If you want to increase your bottom line, creating a great story will help you exponentially. It will help you stand out, and by standing out you will be able to increase your sales. The most important part is understanding this, and developing this story-first mentality. The hard part is crafting the story and then having a great execution for the story.

Chapter 15

Brand Stories to Inspire

In this chapter, I would like to share with you some of my favourite brand stories from our work at way boutique agency, in addition to a few brand stories from further afield.

Over the years we've enhanced the way we tell stories. It's really important to appreciate the 'the right framework for the right story'. As I talked about earlier, it's not about the product, it's not about the service, it's about the goal, the mission. I have compiled a few real-life examples to inspire you, and help you understand more about how I see brand storytelling. Over the next three images you can see how different stories are created.

CENTRAL HOTEL LONDON STORY

> Opening with what we believe in.

Total immersion in a new destination is therapy for the mind, heart and soul. Travel reignites our passions, and restores our spirits; travel is magical.

> The change we want to create.

Travel is magical, but we believe that it shouldn't be a luxury reserved for the few; it should be an essential part of our lives. We want you to explore our city, and its magic, and to explore it deeply, that is our vision.

> The problem.

When we are looking to book a hotel room in London, we want a seamless experience and a comfortable room, without any surprises. We all want a cosy, clean space, with hot water, close to public transport, and friendly people. But it's not always the case, and cool or distant customer service all too common.

> Who we are.

Ours is a family-run business, now by its third generation. It is led by two brothers, Emmanuel and Arthur; the hotel was established by their grandparents when they moved from Malta to London in the 1950s. Emmanuel started working in the hotel just over 35 years ago, when reservations were still received by letter. Arthur joined the business a few years later.

> The solution.

From Central Hotel's doorstep you meet the fresh-faced, vibrant energy of our city. Take a left turn and you will see King's Cross railway station. Featured in many books and films, it is both a landmark of gorgeous, classic Victorian architecture and a contemporary hub, imbued with over 160 years of history. It is also the first step to all that London has to offer.

At Central Hotel, we are dedicated to ensuring our guests have a beautiful experience. We deliver the highest standards for our guests' comfort, helping them to explore more and do more in London.

Explore more. Do more.

HERCULES STORY

What we believe in.

To us, it starts with relentless innovation to give people the priceless feeling of accomplishment for their hard work.

We believe that creation is at the core of all humanity. When we create, we put our energy and our skills on the line. Creation makes the world move.

Making it personal.

Achieving something bigger than yourself is a truly priceless moment that nobody can take away from you. Those memories and emotions are held close to your heart.

The obstacle.

In today's world, it's hard to stand out, the market is crowded, and people are not engaged with brands as they used to be. Sometimes you feel alone trying to fight for visibility in the fog of sound around you. You are trying to gain more attention for your business. You are putting your heart and soul on the line and risking everything you have.

Showing empathy.

We understand the feeling, as we struggled to build and create products that helped us stand out and gain access to the market more than 32 years ago.

Our spirit.

At its core, our team is everything to us; it's everything because without a team that comes together, a team that innovates, we wouldn't be where we are today. We work day and night to achieve the impossible for our clients regardless of how turbulent it can be out there.

Looking for a hero.

People who are relentless and go after their dreams are people that inspire us. They are the ones that spark us to make bold moves and push our limits and go further.

Introducing the hero.

Our clients are those people that truly make a difference; they are the ones that nourish people's lives and give hope to younger generations to keep going, to keep pursuing.

The solution.

At Hercules, we've been creating products that stand out and give a competitive advantage to our customers to say thank you in a more engaging way. With our products, you don't just send a corporate gift; you give something that nobody can take away – and that's the power of a memorable emotion and a joyful moment that will be remembered for a lifetime.

Go Create, Go Innovate.

LAKESIDE HOTEL STORY

Nature around us leaves rustle in the wind. To breathe in a deeply fresh air is rejuvenating to the soul. Everything we want can be found in front of us if we open our eyes and hearts. Nature can help our hearts smile and bring calmness into our chaotic life. It can show us the magic of life.

[Aspiration.] When we travel, we have the opportunity to see things from a new perspective, try new things, generate new ideas, we are able to ignite our curiosity and create something courageous.

[Making it hard for the hero.] Courage comes from the inside, it's an inside job and we believe that courage can be found in every human being.

[The obstacle.] Stress is something that we face on a daily basis. It can discourage us from moving forward and from pursuing our aspirations. We become unmotivated, irritable, we make bad decisions and our racing thoughts constantly make us worry about all the little things. Stress makes us mentally and physically weak.

[Making our guest the hero.] Taking care of others is something that is within your DNA, it's something that you do without considering your needs and wants because this is the kind of a person you are.

[The solution.] At Lakeside Hotel we want to help you put everything aside, leave all your worries behind and provide you with nature at your footsteps. We want to remind your soul that courage is within you.

When you are courageous, you can experience magic all around. You can experience magical memories by taking a long walk along the lake and Frimley Green. You can ignite your curiosity by looking outside the window into the lake and take in the beauty all around you.

Kindly reminded that you are beautiful.

Ignite Your Curiosity

As the client's business develops, some brand stories will evolve. Other stories stay the same. To see and read our latest brand stories, please visit www.way.boutique

You will find lots of the resources there. We explain in detail why there are sentences and words in specific areas, and if you would like to learn more about the stories, just email me on an@way.boutique.

When I have meetings sometimes people ask me about other brands and their stories. What about Louis Vuitton? Or Zappos? How about adidas? Some focus on different aspects in their story, for example luxury brands like Louis Vuitton are on a different level, right? So let's talk about some other brand stories, some that will be more familiar.

Louis Vuitton

The interpretation of "L.V" as "Live" and "Love" reminds customers to live their lives to the fullest and pursue their passion in life, whether it be travelling or simply an important personal journey.

Now, if we look a bit deeper about why is this part of their story, we soon learn that when Louis Vuitton was 16, he made a decision that would not only change his life, but the lives of his sons and future generations. When he came to Paris by foot, he followed his dreams.

Their focus is craftsmanship and creativity, and you can see that in their campaigns and their communications.

Zappos

Since 1999 they have been delivering first-class customer experience; the company's tagline and overarching ethos is to "Deliver Wow". *Delivering Happiness: A Path to Profits, Passion, and Purpose,* tells the story of Zappos from the perspective of someone who knew it best – it is authored by the late, great Tony Hsieh, Zappos' CEO. There are so many stories that I read about Zappos that simply make me say wow! One story in particular that is truly fascinating is the record-breaking 10-hour customer service call. It's actually the opposite of Royal Mail customer service where you can't find a human being to talk to them. Zappos doesn't hurry its customers to just 'get on with the call'. This particular customer service phone call on December 8, 2012 was not even about a complaint. The customer service agent took the time to have a conversation with the caller about living in Las Vegas area which took him 10 hours and 29 minutes. The phone conversation went beyond shoes and it still ended the caller buying a pair of Ugg boots. One customer service agent from Zappos said the following: 'Sometimes people just need to call and talk… We don't judge, we just want to help.'

Think about how these other household names focus and differentiate themselves:

Coca-Cola: To refresh the world. To inspire moments of optimism and happiness.

Disney: We create happiness, by providing the finest in entertainment for people of all ages, everywhere.

Apple: Make tools for the mind that advance humankind.

Google: Organise the world's information and make it universally accessible and useful.

Airbnb: Imagine a world where you can belong anywhere.

Dove: Helping women reconsider and redefine what beauty is.

Monzo: Make money work for everyone.

Lego: Inspire and develop the builders of tomorrow.

We all know some of the bigger brands, and obviously Apple and Nike is always there in every single case study. Here are some companies that you might never heart of.

Brew Dr. Kombucha is a not an average kombucha company. Their brand purpose is sustainability at it's core. And they are not just saying it because it sounds nice, they actually believe in what they do. If you go to their Instagram feed, you will see a colourful background and fun shots of their beverages with graphics that speak about their purpose. Their instragram is a place where you can get educated, and a fun place where you get mocktail recipes and learn more about intersectional environmentalism.

Another great brand is Hanahana Beauty. This brand is on a mission to empower Black women globally. As a skincare and wellness brand, it's mission coincides with handcrafting natural skincare products. On their social media they share stories and updated from The Hanahana Cicrcle of Care – an initiative creative to directly support the women they work with in Ghana.

What happens when you are selling food? Well a great example is Brightland. Their brand purpose according to the founder Aishwarya Iyer is the following: "Brightland was born out of a desire for better, more honest food production – and deep belief in the land and what it provides". Their social media is beautifully crafted with imagery that encourages their community to savor simple moments and nourish their body with locally sourced ingredients. Their whole content on their website and social is stunning, you can see that they put a lot of effort and care into creating it and that they truly believe in what they do.

Another brand with purpose is Boy Smells. They sell candles and intimate wear and according to their founders, they "wanted to have products that were embracing masculine and feminine simultaneously in a simple and straightforward way that wasn't overtly targeted to one gender." They support organizations like The Trevor Project, where they donate 15% of their proceeds from their PRIDE collection to the non-profit. On their Instagram they use influential people from LGBTQIA+ community to create content and educate people about their cause.

Airbnb is asking us to imagine a world where we can belong; Apple is building tools for people with passion who think they can change the world. Great stories don't focus on the product or the service, great stories show how the customer is a hero and the brand is a bridge for the hero to cross and achieve their goal.

Chapter SHHH!

The Five Human Senses

This is a secret chapter. It is also a chapter that will help you triple the emotional connection with your customers. It's a secret chapter because there are some valuable secrets that you can learn and implement. As you realised, creating a brand story is all about creating an emotional connection with your audience but emotional connection is not just about having a story, a slogan, and putting it on the website. You need to execute the story and communicate it with your desired target market.

We have five senses; sight, sound, taste, touch and smell. We all know that. There has been a mountain of research done during the last 30 years about how our five senses influence our decisions to buy.

In the marketing world, when you use the five senses it's called sensory marketing. It means that a business is using all five senses to create a positive impression for their brand. When we appeal to all five senses it helps us gain trust and create a deeper emotional connection.

A lot of high end and luxury brands invest heavily in texture of their napkins, of their menu, of the smell of their place. They spend millions in research and executing this 'small' details; they are not small at all.

Sight. We all know that colours are very important. What I recommend doing is asking your designer or agency why he or she choose your colour scheme. What is the purpose of the colours that you use? Every single colour has feelings attached to it. Different colours imbue different feelings and gives a different feel to the brand. For example, colour yellow equates to optimism, clarity, warmth. The colour red equates to excitement, boldness, and youth. Orange equates to friendly, cheerful, and confident; blue equates to dependability, strength, and trust. The better you understand your brand colour schemes, the better you will appeal to your customers and communicate subconsciously the message about your brand.

With sight you have images, videos and fonts. It's important to choose your style photography, videography and your fonts. It goes back to what you want your customer to think about you. These are important elements that you need to consider.

Voice & Sound.

Do you know how many music songs we have? Millions, one person in a lifetime will not be able to listen to all Spotify playlists. A good question to ask yourself is how would you like your brand to sound? Yes, sound. We all have memories that are connected with certain songs. Think of how would you like your brand to sound.

Jingles. We all know some well-known brand jingles. Think of McDonald's and their 'I'm Loving It' jingle. Once we listen to the first five seconds of the jiggle we immediately know what brand it is from. You don't need to spend $1.37 billion (*Ad Age* May 27, 2015) like McDonald's did on 'I'm Lovin' It', but you can create a nice creative one for less than a thousand pounds.

Taste. This is easy for restaurants, right? They literally sell food. But what kind of taste would be 'a signature' taste for the restaurant? What about for other brands? Well, we need to think of how do we want our customers to feel about our brand? Maybe we want them to think that we are sweet bunch of people. Maybe you use Haribo's or something really sweet that will make them say 'wow, that's so sweet'. Think of something you can use that will be your flagship taste. Maybe it's a specific cookie. The goal is to connect taste and your brand.

Touch. The easiest way to create an impactful touch sensation is with your marketing collateral and your business cards. Large-scale print and design companies like Moo give us so many options when creating business cards and other marketing collateral. You can choose a specific feeling. Yes, you pay a bit extra when you create marketing collateral that stands out, but the conversations you will have will be different. People will comment on things that are unusual. Think of a chocolate brand that has a distinctive packaging that we all know. It's different, it's unique and we all love chocolates, don't we? Did you guess the brand? Tweet or send me a message on any social media @alexnovicov if you guessed it.

Smell. The sense of smell is the most direct link to the brain in human beings. A particular smell can immediately trigger memories and can affect a decision very quickly.

Fragrances and environmental scents can be your choice. You can choose a fragrance that you want the brand to be associated with and spray it on your business cards, or use it for yourself if you meet clients. If you are retail store, restaurant or a hotel you can find a creative way to give that scent to the customer.

You have the five senses that you can use and apply once you create your story. You can decide what you want to use based on your story, so it aligns. You don't need to have thousands of pounds in your budget like luxury hotels and restaurants have. Think how many videos there are on YouTube titled "unboxing ____". People love great packaging, people love things that are different. You have the opportunity to stand out and create a deeper bond with your clients. Think of Apple packaging – when you open one of their boxes it just feels so nice. It feels quality.

There is a lot of talk of 'great customer experience' but 'great' doesn't mean a nice picture. It starts with website design, social media content, messaging – everything should be included. Sensory marketing concept adds value to your customers. And because it adds value it has the potential to increase sales. An example is how Abercrombie & Fitch and Dunkin' Donuts both used sensory marketing to increase sales at one South Korea outlet by 29% (Harvard Business Review, 2015).

Smell is a very powerful sense; there are studies that show that pleasant smells can improve mood by 40%. You can find ways to incorporate scent into your brand, and there are plenty of ideas that you can take and execute.

One of the best customer experiences I had was when I went to a shopping centre to buy shampoo and shower gel. Initially I walked into a Molton Brown store as this is the brand I used to use. When I walked in, nobody greeted me or acknowledged my presence. I decided to try another brand, Rituals. By coincidence they were in the same shopping centre. So I went to their store and loved the whole interior of the store. I loved the fact that they had beautiful sinks where you could try different products, the smell was amazing and after a minute or two a young gentleman came to me with a tray offering some sort of tea in a small paper cup. He explained to me what the tea was and what it does. From that day I've always bought Rituals and I recommended the brand to a couple of my friends and bought some gifts from them. I've been loyal to the brand ever since.

It's not only one element that we need to have. Like with the Rituals example, it's not just because he gave me a small cup of tea, it's the whole experience. The shower gel I'm using right now is in an orange silver container. On it reads "RITUALS OF HAPPY BUDDHA' and below the product name it says 'smile and the world smiles back. Little details matter.

In conclusion, if you connect emotionally and deeply with your customers, they will remember your brand. In return, they will reward you financially.

The secret is out, you can use it. But, please, keep this one to yourself. A lot of small businesses are not taking advantage of it.

Chapter 16

When Walking Away is the Best Thing You Can Do

I have met so many beautiful humans running businesses they were not passionate about. They own the business because of family tradition, or because they've inherited the business and they feel that they have to keep the tradition going.

The truth is that we don't have to do it. Not everybody has the same skill set and not everybody should be doing what their parents and grandparents did. It's 2021, we have so many options right now, we don't need to be stuck in a job we hate, or run a business we do not care about.

Sometimes we lose our passion for what we do. It has certainly happened to me. Once, I was thinking of giving up the agency and doing something else. I had lost my passion.

Then, I had a realisation; I realised that I could focus on doing the right thing, focus on adding value and finding the right people for the right shoes and, at the

When Walking Away is the Best Thing You Can Do

same time, inspire them. Perhaps you can inspire people to be more confident, and remind them that they are enough, maybe you can inspire people to dress better, to improve their taste, to help them understand more.

When I was thinking about giving up marketing, I looked to Seth Godin's work. I thought to myself, 'The guy is brilliant; he is making a positive change, he doesn't manipulate, he doesn't sell a fake story.' Then I remembered that there are other brands out there that truly care about their product and their customers, I remembered that there are people like you, who love what they do, and want to spread a message about their products and services. I did not need to give up marketing – I could do the opposite, and instead learn all I can about the human brain, I can learn why we behave a certain way, and learn about storytelling. I can learn and use my skills to help others achieve their goals, and hopefully together we can change our society, our culture, just a tiny bit. I know that, perhaps, I will not change the world, but I know that I can change myself, and I know that, maybe, somebody can be inspired by the actions I take, and move forward to make a bigger impact.

Philip Morris purposely deceived the public when marketing an addictive product (United States vs Philip Morris). Naked Juice claimed that their juices were 'all natural' until it was challenged in court. They had to pay nine million US dollars in action lawsuit. The dairy industry is trying to convince people that milk is healthy, it's a lie but they still try.

The meat industry is trying to convince people to eat meat as it's a tradition and we need protein, it's a huge lie and propaganda but they still do it.

Sure, we can keep on doing what we are doing, because the customer keeps telling the story about that purchase. Or we can change: we can educate our customers, we can make things happen for the better. The choice is ours.

What I recommend is to pause and reflect for a week, or a month, and truly ask 'What difference do I make with my business?' If you don't have a good answer, sell the business and start something else. Start something that will make a difference, because otherwise it's really not worth it. Even if you can't afford a business, you can make some sort of agreement. More than 10 years ago, I ran a business, a retail kiosk shop, where I didn't buy the business because I didn't have the funds, but I managed it with a contract. There is always a solution. Sometimes it's hard, sometimes it's really hard, but I'm a believer that if we want to achieve something we can, we can achieve it, there is always a *way*.

Consider dating, marriage and divorce. You meet somebody, you fall in love, you are in a relationship,

When Walking Away is the Best Thing You Can Do

you get married, but then after a few years, you outgrow each other, and you realise that you are not compatible anymore. You see, most people think that love is the most important thing. I don't agree with this idea; love is important, but it's not the most important thing, because if two people are not compatible with each other – if two people don't see the world the same or at least in a similar way – then it won't last. I loved all of my exes, but with some we weren't compatible and with others it was the wrong time.

My point is that, sometimes, you outgrow a business or the business outgrows you. It's okay to make a change, it's okay to say that you have had enough. Our time is limited on this planet - why waste it, or wait until you go into retirement to do something you truly want to do? I'm a student of Stoic philosophy and one of my favourite quotes is by Marcus Aurelius:

"Don't behave as if you are destined to live forever. What's fated hangs over you. As long as you live and while you can, become good now."

Another quote by Epictetus should inspire us to demand the best of ourselves today, right now:

"How long are you going to wait before you demand the best for yourself?"

I always say that we need to find what we want to struggle for. If we want to grow mentally, spiritually, we need to push ourselves. Happiness is not watching Netflix or buying things; happiness is the process of achieving something. Have you noticed that when we buy that new thing we wanted we are 'happy' for a few minutes, hours, or a day, perhaps, and then we feel empty again? That's because we got our dopamine hit and then want more. That's why the best thing to do is to train ourselves to want less, and to use things, rather let things control us.

When we have a purpose, when we live on purpose, we wake up every morning and we feel different, we feel that we have so many things that we want to do, not *have* to do but *want* to do. There is a huge difference. People with purpose see the bigger picture: they see a problem and they see themselves as being a part of the solution. They wake up inspired – not every day, some days are bad days, some days are rainy days, but some days are great days. When we live with passion, we inspire others around us to live with passion, to do creative work, to push our boundaries – and this is how we change our culture, this is how we improve society. When we live with passion, we live in the present moment, we are truly present in what is happening right now. Yesterday is the past, and tomorrow is not certain. The only certain thing we have is this, right now. All we have is now.

I always say that you don't have to be the best designer, but the goal is to *aim to become* the best designer, the best storyteller, the best coffee maker, the best chef, the best piano player, the best artist, and keep on going, keep on moving. It's not about competing against others, but instead working together and working to improve things. When we are working on improving our products, our services, ourselves, we send a positive energy out there, we send, as they say, 'good vibes' to the world. This doesn't mean that everything is easy, or that we have an easy life living by the beach in Cyprus or Spain.

Once we find our purpose, then we start looking at the world in a different way. We stop paying attention to drama, we stop scrolling on social media, we stop wasting time, and we start living in the present moment, or at least become aware when we are not present and train our minds to live in the present moment.

I believe we have got to the end of this book. This has been a journey. I wrote this version of the book a couple of times - actually four times – and I rewrote this book from scratch twice. And here we are - if you are reading this, it means it's the final version.

I would like to thank you very much for being on this journey with me, for reading this book, for buying this book and finishing it. I'm extremely grateful for you and if I can help you in any way, you can write to me at an@way.boutique and I will gladly assist you and be there for you. Last year, 2020, was a hard year due to COVID-19, but like any difficulties we have faced as humans, we overcome them by looking forward and doing what we can do today. Many industries were adversely affected, but you know what? It makes us stronger, much stronger.

It's time to create your story.

About the Author

Alexander Novicov believes in creating a world where people live with passion, and go beyond their own expectations.

He is a human, a public speaker, a runner, an author, an animal lover, a storyteller, and he runs a boutique agency called way – a brand purpose and content marketing agency. An agency that is on a mission to help people that care about what they do to flourish.

Alexander has worked with some brilliant brands since the inception of the agency in November 2010. These include Stella Artois, Holland & Barrett, Eurovision, T.G.I Fridays, Beautyline, Central Hotel London and many others. He has also spoken at different events around the world. To name a few: HOW Festival in Croatia, Hotel Technology Innovation in Dubai, Digital Marketing Advertising in Cyprus,

Business Show in Olympia London and others. University of Greenwich, University of Nicosia and other educational establishments have benefited from his talks.

In a nutshell, Alexander Novicov is on a mission to help people with passion go beyond.

Acknowledgments

I am thankful I did not give up, and for writing this book despite all my insecurities and the challenges that I faced. I'm very lucky to have some wonderful people in my life that I can call friends and family. I would like to thank my mum, Tania, who believed in me, and my dad, Iuri– a huge thanks to him for being for who he is, and for being there for me. My grandfather – who still doesn't understand what I do, but always listens to me very quietly. I would like to thank my brother from another mother Michalis Schizas. Mrs Maria Schizas and Mr Andreas Schizas for being like a family to me. Of course, I can't thank enough Mrs Roulla Iacovidou for being my second mum when I was young.

Zenon Zindilis, for being a fantastic friend since I was 16 years old. Marcos Komodromos, for being a beautiful friend. Emmanuel Caruana for believing in me and trusting me when I first came to his hotel, and being such a great friend for the past years, you will never know the impact you made to my life. Arthur Caruana for being one of the kindest humans

I know – thank you for believing in me and thank you for being such a lovely friend, I'm truly grateful for you Arthur. Sam Leonard for being a great friend and inviting me to a conference that has changed the trajectory in my life in 2018. My team at way boutique agency, including our designer, Louiza Ainsley.

I can't thank enough all the clients that have and still are working with us, without you, none of this would be possible. I'm truly grateful to every single one of you.

This book was inspired by a lot of great people I haven't met in person, but definitely inspired me to push myself, including Seth Godin, Gary Vaynerchuk, Simon Sinek, Bernadette Jiwa and many other fantastic authors and marketers.

Adios!
Αντίο!
до свидания!

Further reading

Story Proof: The Science Behind the Startling Power of Story by Hendall Haven

Start with Why: How Great Leaders Inspire Everyone to Take Action by Simon Sinek

The Purple Cow: Transform Your Business by Being Remarkable by Seth Godin

All Marketers Are Liars: The Power of Telling Authentic Stories in a Low-Trust World, also by Seth Godin

Sell With A Story by Paul Smith

Delivering Happiness: A Path to Profits, Passion, and Purpose by Tony Hsieh

Selfie: How We Became So Self-obsessed and What It's Doing to Us by Will Storr

The Science of Storytelling, also by Will Storr

The Thank You Economy by Gary Vaynerchuk

The Brand Gap by Marty Neumier

References

Here are all the references that I made in this book, all the data, all the research that I've pointed out.

CHAPTER 2

Accenture Research purpose driven: https://www.businesswire.com/news/home/20181205005061/en/Majority-Consumers-Buying-Companies-Stand-Issues-Care

Cone/Porter Novelli Purpose Study:
https://www.conecomm.com/research-blog/2018-purpose-study

CHAPTER 5

How Stories Affect Our Brain: https://www.thinglink.com/scene/891368436381253633

CHAPTER 7

Microsoft 2000 Study On Attention Span: https://about.ads.microsoft.com/en-us/insights/stories/intelligent-connections

References

Dave Trott Data: https://davetrott.co.uk/2008/04/why-do-we-assume-people-have-to-like-adverts/

A study from the Technical University of Denmark on attention span: https://www.theguardian.com/society/2019/apr/16/got-a-minute-global-attention-span-is-narrowing-study-reveals

Media Post: https://www.mediapost.com/publications/article/340946/data-estimates-40-of-all-media-spend-is-wasted-.html

How Away Brings Its Brand To Life through content marketing:
https://insights.newscred.com/away-content-marketing/

CHAPTER 10

Huel Revenue:
https://find-and-update.company-information.service.gov.uk/company/07907551/filing-history

CHAPTER 12

Veganuary data:
https://www.vegansociety.com/news/media/statistics

CHAPTER SHHH!

Sensory Marketing:https://hbr.org/2015/03/the-science-of-sensory-marketing

Scent Can Improve Mood By 40%:
https://us.moodmedia.com/scent/scent-research/

McDonalds Spend $1.37 billion on 'I'm Loving It' Jingle:https://adage.com/article/cmo-strategy/apple-beats-google-top-spot-global-brand-ranking/298769

CHAPTER 13

Shopping For Christmas 2020: https://www.retailresearch.org/shopping-for-christmas.html

The last, huge thank you is to you, the reader. I would like to thank you from the bottom of my heart for taking the time and reading this book. I truly appreciate it.

More information:

If you would like to know more and follow what way is up to, then please do head to way.boutique for the agency things and alexnovicov.com to find more information and insights. You can sign up to my newsletter at alexnovicov.com/friends where I share interesting ideas and thoughts. You can also find me on all social media with my username @alexnovicov. I would love to connect with you, send me a tweet or a message and let's meet up.

Again, thank you and be great.

Alexander Novicov

Lightning Source UK Ltd.
Milton Keynes UK
UKHW021850040821
388290UK00007B/209